j. thomas trimble

Silver in the Psalms

"... like silver seven times refined"
—PSALM 12:6. TLB

Broadman Press/Nashville, Tennessee

Dedication

To my parents, Gus and Elsie Trimble
To my wife I'lee and her parents
Howard and Frances Barnes
And to my children
Sherry, John, and Vince

© Copyright 1976 · Broadman Press
All rights reserved
4251-39
ISBN: 0-8054-5139-0

All Scripture passages, unless otherwise credited, are from
The Living Bible, Paraphrased (Wheaton: Tyndale House
Publishers, 1971) and are used by special permission of the
Publishers.

Subject headings: BIBLE. O. T. PSALMS
Dewey Decimal Classification: 223.2
Library of Congress Catalog Card Number: 75-35396
Printed in the United States of America

PART ONE

Origins of
Silver in the Psalms

A. The Challenge

Silver in the Psalms is a highly personal book. I have tried to put in written form what has been for me a meaningful devotional experience. I want to share it with those I love and those to whom I am closest.

The origins of the book lie in my own personal experience in Bible devotional reading in the Psalms. When I have needed to receive comfort, encouragement, confidence, inspiration, courage, etc., I have often turned to the Psalms in an effort to meet my need. Because I had become rather familiar with several specific places in the Psalms—where I knew in advance I could receive the spiritual uplifting I sought—I was able to go directly to some special passage, there to receive the spiritual nourishment I needed for my sagging soul.

For example, when I have wanted to remind myself of the value of living the virtuous Christian life, I could turn to the first Psalm and read: "Blessed is the man who walketh not in the counsel of the ungodly, nor standeth in the way of sinners, nor sitteth in the seat of the scornful. But his delight is in the law of the Lord, and in his law doth he meditate day and night. And he shall be like a tree planted by the rivers of water that bringeth forth his fruit in his season. His leaf also shall not wither; and whatsoever he doeth shall prosper" (1:1-3, KJV). These words would often be exactly what I needed to encourage my soul, so I could continue with confidence my Christian walk.

On another occasion perhaps, when I might have been feeling particularly awed by a magnificent sunset, and felt the desire to reach out and touch God in my soul, I could turn to Psalm 19 and there read: "The heavens declare the glory of God, and the firmament showeth his handiwork. Day unto day uttereth [its] speech, and night unto night showeth [his] knowledge. There is no speech nor language where their voice is not heard. Their line [message] is gone out through all the earth, and their words to the end of the world" (19:1-4, KJV). After reading such a passage, I would feel especially close to God.

Again perhaps, when the death angel had trodden through my peaceful valley, leaving behind fearful goblins of gloom, spectres of loneliness, and the relentless awareness of unending loss, I would want to run and throw open the pages of the Bible, turning to Psalm 23, almost greedily to gulp in the words: "The Lord is my shepherd, I shall not want. He maketh me to lie down in green pastures; he leadeth me beside the still waters; he restoreth my soul. He leadeth me in the paths of righteousness for his name's sake. Yea though I walk through the valley of the shadow of death, I will fear no evil, for thou art with me. Thy rod and staff they comfort me" (23:1-4, KJV). There are no words to express the feelings of release I would experience after having read a passage like this.

A final example may suffice. On those occasions when I desperately needed cleansing forgiveness of my sins through the grace of God, I knew I could turn, with tears of sorrow and repentence, to Psalm 51 and gratefully read:

"Have mercy upon me, O God, according to thy lovingkindness—according unto the multitude of thy tender mercies blot out my transgressions. Wash me thoroughly from mine iniquity and cleanse me from my sin. For I acknowledge my transgressions, and my sin is ever before me. Against thee—thee only have I sinned, and done this evil in thy sight—that thou mightest be justified when thou speakest, and be clear when thou judgest . . . . Purge me . . . . and I shall be clean: wash me, and I shall be whiter than snow. Make me to hear joy and gladness; . . . create in me a clean heart, O God, and renew a right spirit within me . . . . Restore unto me the joy of thy salvation and uphold me with thy free spirit" (51:1-4, 7-8, 10, 12, KJV).

The healing I would experience through reading that psalm was effective and total. These, then, are the kinds of experiences representative of what I received from the Scripture when I turned in my need to specific passages with which I was acquainted. They fulfilled my expectation and met my immediate need.

However, if I had a different kind of need, I would experience something quite different. Occasionally I felt like reading in the Psalms as if to surprise myself with some unexpected source of spiritual blessing. In this way, I would read in an exploratory way to see how God might bless me— as though putting myself into the hands of the Holy Spirit, assuming a passive, receptive frame of mind, and letting God speak to me as he would. If this kind of devotional reading were my purpose, I found that for me it was a most difficult goal to attain. It was far more difficult than if I knew in advance pretty much what I wanted spiritually, and then went directly to some psalm which I knew— through previous experience—contained what I might very likely need.

But I want to underscore the point that the kind of reading I refer to here is *not* analytical Bible study. Rather, I am talking about devotional reading, particularly the kind of exploring which seeks to uncover new, yet undiscovered sources of inspiration in parts of the Psalms with which one is not as familiar as he is with the more popular Psalms. And so, with *these* particular kinds of goals in mind, I found that all too often in my devotional reading I was unable to fulfill my hopes of receiving a blessing. I became stuck in an impasse. What was the trouble?

Upon reflection, I came to the conclusion that the problem lay in the way the Psalms were arranged due to the nature of the Psalms. I see the Psalms of the Bible as song-poems which reflect the struggles and joys the writers experienced as they tried to understand what happened to them in this world and in the light of their faith in God.

Some psalms exult in victory and reveal the expression of euphoria. In the reading of these psalms it is obvious that the psalmist sees a clear and distinct connection between his human experience and the working of God's will and way in the world. Other psalms, however, express confusion, consternation, disappointment, guilt, anger, frustration, vindictiveness, and many other negative emotions. In these psalms we detect a definite feeling on the part of the psalmist that there is a disconnectedness between his life experiences and the way he has perceived God's will to be working in the world. And so the Psalms present to us a picture of mixed emotional expression. Sometimes the same emotional theme runs throughout a psalm (positive or negative), but more often there are one or more swings of mood within the same psalm.

It seems to me that it is precisely because the book of Psalms contains a great number of psalms which express doubt and consternation about the meaning of God's will in human experience—and also express other negative, but very human emotions—that they are so convincingly real.

It is the unanswered questioning, most of the time coupled with faith, which gives the Psalms their intensely human appeal, I believe. We can all understand and accept the operation of the will of God when it coincides with our wishes and needs. But the waters become muddy when what is apparently God's will turns out to be so opposite to what we had wanted. That is puzzling indeed!

I discovered, then, that it was because of the nature of the Psalms themselves, and the fact that the full range of human emotion is scattered throughout the Psalms, that I was unable to obtain the spiritual fruit I sought *when* I read the Scriptures, nondirectedly, and with the limited goal in mind of receiving only positive spiritual nourishment. This seemed to be the cause of my problem as I tried to meet a special kind of devotional need.

Let me now elaborate on the distinction I am making between the two different approaches to Bible devotions in the Psalms. As we read the Psalms, we are able to appreciate how great a gift God has given us in the Psalms. We are able to see there humanity struggling with many of the same problems we face today. Consequently, we can easily project ourselves into the psalmists' feelings. We experience a feeling of oneness with them across the centuries. We identify personally with their sufferings and their glories and, thereby, reap immense personal benefits here and now in the persistent present. Yes, the Psalms, as they are written, offer us much for our Christian growth.

If a person, however, would like to enter the Psalms, attempting to restrict the range of his emotional identification to positive feelings, he is likely to encounter serious obstacles blocking his path to that goal. It would not be long at all until he would come across material irrelevant to his specific purpose. If a person needed, at *that* particular time in his life, to receive a special kind of gift from God in the Psalms—a gift of consolation, encouragement, hope, inspiration, confidence, or the courage to go on—then he would, in all likelihood, not be able to obtain his blessing without wading through many passages which would not be in line with his purpose.

Let me illustrate what I mean, and show how this might happen. Let us suppose, for example, that a person were feeling doubtful, for some reason, about the love, the kindness, the mercy of God, and suppose he sought to find again his confidence that God does care for him and love him. He has chosen, let us assume, to encourage himself by reading nondirectedly in the Psalms, hoping to come across something which would bless his soul and meet his special needs on that occasion.

He begins reading. It would not be unlikely that he might, very soon in his reading happen upon passages very similar to the following, rather pointed selection: "And he will slap them in the face, insulting them and breaking off their teeth" (3:7); "May all who hate the Jews be brought to ignominious defeat" (129:5); "The wicked are the scum you skim off and throw away" (119:119); "Let no one be kind to him; let no one pity his fatherless children. May they die. May his family name be blotted out in a single generation" (109:12-13); "We die beneath your anger; we are overwhelmed by your wrath" (90:7); "Destroy them! Cover them with failure and disgrace—these enemies of mine" (71:13); "His people must destroy them. Cover your feet with their blood; dogs will eat them" (68:23); "They shouted for help but no one dared rescue them; they cried to the Lord, but he refused to answer them. So I crushed them fine as dust and cast them to the wind. I threw them away like sweepings from the floor" (18:41-42).

A person with the goals in mind I have described would find little comfort in these passages.

Not only do the Psalms, as they are presently arranged, contain little possibility for the specific kind of edification I

12

have described, but also very often they could even stop the individual in his tracks, spoiling his effort to obtain the special kind of blessing he needs and is so desperately searching for.

Occasionally, this very thing *has* happened to me. It was at these times that I disappointedly reflected that: it would certainly be a bountiful blessing if, on those special occasions when I only wanted to be washed with the water of the Word—rather than to be scalded—there would be available a version of the Psalms which contained only those passages of Scripture which might have the greatest possibility to meet my special kind of need at that time— a collection of psalm selections which did not contain those passages which I had found in the past to have deflected me from my devotional purpose.

These, then, where the kinds of experiences I had in devotional Bible reading, and the gist of the thoughts and fantasies which went through my mind and became the seedbed for *Silver in the Psalms.* The concept underlying the book originated in a personal experience I had in trying to meet my devotional needs in the Psalms .

B. A Solution: Silver in the Psalms

For years I had thought that I wanted to do something special with the Psalms, which would make it easy for a person to obtain the rich spiritual treasures which lay there. Years ago a title for such a work suggested itself to me. It seemed to feel exactly right for whatever work I might do, should God ever lead me to do it. The title was and is *Silver in the Psalms.* I felt that this title faithfully mirrored my conviction that the precious gems of comfort which lay in the Psalms could be even more creatively mined and refined to help others receive even greater payloads of blessings than they were now able to receive. But only recently did God provide me with the technological insight concerning how I might put together my devotional dream.

There were problems and personal obstacles to overcome before I was to construct this version. I didn't want to produce just an additional commentary on the Psalms—there were already many excellent works like that available. Anyway, I felt personally uncomfortable suggesting to others how they should understand the Scriptures. I felt ill at ease in the role of explaining to a reader what some passage was attempting to say at deeper levels of meaning. The less obvious the interpretation, the more uncomfortable I felt. This was a personal feeling of mine about myself—not about what others should do. And so I didn't want to do a work in the traditional area. No, what I wanted to do was entirely different.

Also, the fact that I was going to *select* for inclusion in my work certain parts of the Psalms gave me some problems. The fact was that whenever I selected some particular passage for inclusion in my collection, I was at the same time necessarily excluding other passages. Who was I, I asked myself, to choose for someone else passages which I felt might bless them? This troubled me. Then I came slowly to the growing and strong conviction that the work had to be a most personal work. Only in this way could I feel comfortable in presenting to others what I felt might maximize their chances of meeting devotional needs of the kind I have described. I had to choose only for myself and then offer to share my blessing with others.

I also found that I had to struggle with some rather old and deeply entrenched persuasions I had accepted totally and without question in years gone by. These ideas, deeply intertwined with old feelings, had to be dealt with before I could permit myself to do the work. One thing that bothered me was the fact that I had always been taught never, under any circumstance, to exclude Scripture—for any reason. That sounded right to me when I first heard

14

it, but as often is the case, I swallowed the words without chewing the meaning. I had to work on what I felt about these matters before I could write the book.

Another obstacle blocking my path was my original personality tendency to be somewhat uncomfortable with feelings, but right at home with thoughts. I was not that I didn't like feeling, nor that I didn't experience feeling; nor was it that I was not a "feeling" person; it was rather that I had been trained all my life to be a thinking person.

It had been strongly implied to me, and sometimes directly taught, that feelings were a little unstable, somewhat unreliable, and yes, perhaps even dangerous! So, when these attitudes were taught to me—if not *taught to* me, then certainly *caught by* me—they found a hospitable ally in the cultural training I had received from society. I was taught to be primarily a thinking person!

These attitudes, which I learned as I grew up, I now view as false. They succeeded only in making me half a person! We are thinking-feeling persons. So I had to reach the place in my development where I could learn to trust my feelings before I could write the work. This was because I was going to rely so heavily upon feeling to write *Silver in the Psalms*.

I also had to confront an objection I knew some would inevitably have with my work. I am aware that some might say that we will always receive exactly what we need from the Scriptures when we read them, whether or not we are aware of that need as we begin our reading. God will see to that. I do not at all dispute the fact that, as it is true with prayer, so it often is with devotional Bible reading. If it is true that, "We know not what we should pray for as we ought" (Rom. 8:26, KJV), it is also likely to be true that we know not what we need when we read the Bible. God often does surprise us with an unexpected blessing coming from a direction we did not expect. Yet, I do not feel it follows that we should never make an effort to arrange the Scriptures

15

in meaningful ways for specific, albeit limited, purposes.

If such an approach is incorrect, then, Bible studies which gather related material from various parts of the Bible for a topical study of some subject should likewise seem to be an invalid approach. No, in my mind the arrangement of the Scriptures into topical collections by the minister as he reads Scripture to the people, and the use of congregational responsive readings from the Bible are little different from the approach I have used in this book. Passages are gathered from various places in the Scriptures around a central theme in the two examples I have cited, and *Silver in the Psalms* also represents the same sort of effort to select passages from the Psalms into a collection for a special devotional purpose. I feel comfortable with that. But that was an issue I had to face if I were to be sensitive to the feelings of some persons who might have trouble with the innovative kind of approach of *Silver in the Psalms*.

II. A Rationale for the Arrangement

A. An Affective Approach

I wanted to construct an arrangement of passages which would help a person meet *one* particular type of devotional need, an arrangement which would contain only relatively positive and hopeful passages. Yet, I wanted to avoid the suggestion that my own collection of passages was the *only* possible way to accomplish such a goal, or that it was the *best* possible selection of Psalm-passages. So, I reasoned that the work would have to be a highly personal one. This would leave everyone free to like or dislike my choices. It seemed to follow, in my mind, that such a personal version could best be accomplished by using as the selective principle a guide which was uniquely mine— *my feelings*. Feelings are not true or false—they simply are.

16

In this way, my choice of passages could not be evaluated on the basis of whether the choices were correct or incorrect, but rather on the basis of whether or not they met a person's spiritual needs. That was exactly what I wanted. I can understand that some may read the collection and feel that neither the collection nor the approach is for them, that the work does not speak to their spiritual need, that it does not speak to them where they are in their quest for spiritual enrichment. I have no quarrel with such feelings.

Each person is an expert on his own needs and wants. He has the right to seek the fulfillment of his needs and wants in ways and places that are most meaningful to him. My book is not for those persons. My book is for the person who, upon reading the collection of passages, finds increased spiritual nourishment and senses a kinship with my feelings and a fellowship with my needs and wants.

So, I decided to construct an affective—a feeling—version of the Psalms, one based upon my own private feelings and reactions. In this way I could construct a selection which would meet my own personal devotional needs, and at the same time leave everyone else entirely free to react to my selection either with: "This particular selection of passages from this psalm really does meet my needs very well, and if I were to select passages myself, I probably would select about the same ones"; or they would be equally free to say, "This selection is not what I need at all—I need something much different from the passages selected."

How does one go about putting together an arrangement of psalms based primarily upon feeling rather than some rational principle, such as gathering together all Scripture dealing with: heaven, historical statements, prophetic statements, or messianic statements? These rationally-based examples I have mentioned are easily recognizable as those things which might appear in a topical handbook or in a concordance arranged topically.

My approach was to avoid thinking about *how* to go about accomplishing such a task (which only plays into the hands of reason, thus defeating the whole purpose in the first place). I just began reading, listening to my feelings and reacting as to whether or not the passage I was reading was producing positive emotional responses in me—generally "good feelings." Or whether I was experiencing blocking, irrelevance, thwarting, frustration, questioning, or anything else which would keep me from receiving what I needed to deal with now-problems involving my now-feelings.

I am finding it a little difficult even now to put into words how I used my feelings to select the passages, but, then, that is the nature of feelings. They are experienced and validated subjectively, and then communicated more nonverbally than verbablly. Feelings which don't fit" leave a person feeling uncomfortable, and somehow experiencing irresolution and incompleteness. I have usually found that when I experience feelings of discomfort, it is because my head (my reasoning) and my heart (my feelings) are not together—not in accord. For example, I may have what I think at first sight is a good idea and consider implementing it. But if I experience an uneasiness, I try to listen to my feelings and to take a second look at the supposed "good idea." Many times I find that I had overlooked something; my "heart" had perceived it, although my mind had not. In these instances I was saved from a mistake by being aware of my feelings. At times the heart knows what, of which the mind knows naught.

But it works the other way, too. Sometimes I have had a definite feeling about something, a feeling so clear that I could not deny I experienced it, but somehow that feeling "did not compute"—it did not "fit." Upon closer inspection (heightened awareness), I often discovered that my feeling, although definitely there, was an invalid one—one I knew I did not want to continue experiencing, because it had no right to exist in me. It was a persisting feeling, carried over

18

from many years ago—sometimes from my childhood—which had no reason for continued existence. It could only result in a neurotic, distorted way of looking at or dealing with the world.

In this case my mind had acted as a check upon my feelings and had reminded me that there was no place for such feelings in me. The feeling had a right to be overridden, to be "defused" of its strength, to be denounced as having no legitimate claim to remain a part of my being. Old prejudices are further examples of such antiquated feelings identified by our reason as stupid spectres of insanity, fully deserving to have their disrespectable robes torn from them.

So, my approach was to read and to feel, not to think or to question. I began to read, starting with Psalm 1, and to select what felt warm or what brought forth caring feelings of empathy within me for the feelings of the psalmist. What did not "set well" I put aside, at least for the time being, with no questions asked. That would come later, but not now. And so with feelings out front, and thought submerged into the background, I continued to read.

The feeling-response I tried to make to the Scriptures was as primitive and as pure as I could manage. That is, I tried to react personally to the words and thoughts as I perceived them, rather than to react on the basis of some kind of theological interpretation of the passage. I am sure that the theological teachings I have received through the years did, to some extent, creep through to influence my feeling-response to the passages. Because of that, I worked hard to minimize the influence, or at least to keep the influence general, rather than to permit it to become a focused filter through which all feeling flowed. I do feel I was able to accomplish this to an appreciable extent. On the basis, then, of this highly personalized feeling approach, I have described my work as an "affective"—a feeling—version of the Psalms.

19

B. The Rationale and Strategy of Implementation

After the whole process of selection had been completed, having used primarily my feelings as a guide, I wanted to use my intellect to see if I could discern the principles which had guided my feelings. I wanted to do this both as an exercise in self-awareness and as a means of communicating to others the principles I had used in my selection process. In this way I could exercise the double check I alluded to previously. After having "lost my mind and having come to my senses" as Fritz Perls, the founder of Gestalt therapy used to say—I wanted to check out, with my mind reclaimed, what had come to my senses.

But I think I should clarify a point here. The use of my feelings, as opposed to the use of my intellect, was certainly not so distinct and differentiated a process that the use of either was one of pure feeling only or the use of uncontaminated intellect. Of course, it was always a combination of both. No one is so divided that he can completely shut off any part of himself. I only maintain that the process through which I went was primarily *dominated* either by feelings or by intellect, and that the effort to try to be *"blind"* to the other mode of functioning was a conscious one.

As I look back upon my creative process, the impression I receive is one of inclusion rather than exclusion. Nearly every psalm has passages included in my collection, and most of them have generous portions included. My overall, general purpose was not to exclude, but to include. I looked at each passage with the question, "Can I keep this?"

What, then, were the principles of inclusion I used? I discovered a few major inclusion principles and some minor ones, too. The major selection principle, I suppose, was the inclusion of all passages which were definite statements of encouragement, comfort, security, repose, trust, praise, re-

20

joicing, and other such positively-toned passages. I also utilized another selection principle, which resulted in my retaining several somewhat negatively-toned passages of a particular kind.

I did in fact select passages which reflected sorrow, repentance, regret, feelings of guilt and remorse, sadness, and even depression. For example, what could feel more "negative" in one sense of the word than the passage in Psalm 51: 1-4: "O loving and kind God, have mercy. Have pity upon me and take away the awful stain of my transgressions. Oh, wash me, cleanse me from this guilt. Let me be pure again. For I admit my shameful deed—it haunts me day and night. It is against you and you alone I sinned, and done this terrible thing. You saw it all, and your sentence against me is just."

What negatively-toned feelings might arise in a reader through the following passage, in Psalm 69:1-3? "Save me O my God. The floods have risen. Deeper and deeper I sink in the mire; the waters rise around me. I have wept until I am exhausted; my throat is dry and hoarse; my eyes are swollen with weeping, waiting for my God to act." The voice of despair is unmistakable.

Consider another passage. Frustration is plain in the words of the psalmist in Psalm 73:13-14: "Have I been wasting my time? Why take the trouble to be pure? All I get out of it is trouble and woe—every day and all day long!"

Those passages are all negative in one sense, yet they have a redeeming quality to them. They are capable of resolution. The same may be said for other similarly included passages such as in Psalms 86:1, 88:1-3 and 9, 90:5-6, most of Psalm 107, and 119:28. In these psalms, although the psalmist felt sadness and a cast-down spirit, the spiritual condition was used as a means to receive encouragement and to lift up his eyes with hope of redemption.

The kind of negative passages which I did not include in

21

my collection certainly reflected very valid human conditions, also: anger, bitterness, resentment, disillusionment, frustration, envy, jealousy, pride, condescension, vindictiveness, superiority, provincialism, belligerency, self-aggrandizement, grandiosity, suspicion, and ethnocentrism. However, these emotions and orientations I judged to be much more corrosive and self-defeating. There was a poison within them which seemed to have no redemptive quality. The Psalms contain a fairly large dosage of these very human attributes, and as I said before, this may be a part of the reason the Psalms are so real to us—they present to us persons who experience the full range of human emotion—the good and the ugly. But these kinds of emotions were not in line with my devotional purposes and, thus, were not included.

I should express myself at this point about what I feel is the most productive use of the passages which do contain the more corrosive human emotions. The Psalms do present to us a picture of the full range of human emotions. Yet, for us to identify emotionally with these feelings to the extent that we would ever point to their occurrence in the Psalms as a justification for harboring them in ourselves, or to speak of them as useful human emotions, would seem to amount to a blind rationalization—the purpose of which would be to maintain totally undesirable human traits within us.

I do not feel that bitterness, resentment, vindictiveness, sarcasm, envy, jealousy, etc., have any place in the mentally healthy Christian personality. For example, if a person were to read some of the imprecatory Psalms, and then find himself feeling somewhat euphoric and identifying rather strongly with the punishment to others which is being expressed in these particular psalms, this should call for some real soul-searching on his part. These psalms exist the way they do for a reason, but not that they might be emulated.

My own personal feeling is that they are there to remind

us that biblical heroes can also have feet of clay. Although there may be some occasions when one would want to read such passages, the occasions would be relatively fewer compared to the times a person would want to read in the Psalms to meet the kind of needs my work is designed to fulfill. Thus, they are not included in my collection.

As I continued to assess what I had attempted to do in the preparation of *Silver in the Psalms,* I became aware that I had also been implementing an important psychological principle, one which would enhance our ability to let the Psalms speak to us *in the here and now.* One important principle of human behavior which is often utilized by skilled counselors is the principle of ambiguity. Roughly, the principle states that the more ambiguous (unstructured, unorganized, unclear) a situation is when presented to a person for his response, the more likely it is that he will project himself into the ambiguous stimulus situation and see himself there. A skilled psychotherapist, by using the principle of ambiguity, can help a person become aware of parts of himself he has projected into some "neutral" (ambiguous) stimulus presented to him.

For example, there are few more ambiguous stimulus presentations than the Rorschach inkblots, a widely-used instrument employed by psychologists to help a person learn more about himself. The inkblots are just that—blots of ink and nothing more—but people find different things in those blots. Of course, the blots do lend themselves to several fairly common or typical interpretations, but these are well-known and there is much room left to permit a person to project much of his personality onto the inkblots for interpretation by the therapist.

This principle of ambiguity, I realized *post hoc,* has been employed in the construction of *Silver in the Psalms.* The technique I have used has increased the ambiguity of the Psalms, it has made them more general, and so widely ap-

23

plicable, that almost anyone could see his own experience in the passage he was reading. This was accomplished by eliminating nearly everthing that was so concrete and specific that it could not possibly apply to a reader's own life—unless perhaps the reader were able to make an extremely broad interpretation or comparison of the very specific passage to something in his own life.

Skilled Bible interpreters and Bible teachers are well-trained to make this kind of generalization, but most laypersons are not. It is not because of any lack of ability on the part of the layperson, but because of a lack of knowledge about specific facts which lie behind the situation read about—often in the history or culture of the persons about whom the passage is speaking. Laypersons usually have not had access to that kind of information.

Let me illustrate the kind of very concrete passage I did not include for the reasons I have mentioned above. "Let him reign from sea to sea, and from the Euphrates River to the ends of the earth. The desert nomads shall bow before him; his enemies shall fall face downward in the dust. Kings along the Mediterranean coast—the kings of Tarshish and the islands—and those from Sheba and from Seba—all will bring their gifts" (Ps. 72:9-10). Few persons could project themselves with their personal problems into this kind of passage. It is useful, but for other purposes than the purposes of this work.

Such a passage as the one quoted speaks again for the value of the study of the Psalms from an analytical point of view, under the guidance of a skilled Bible teacher and/or a good Bible commentary; but the ordinary layperson, without access to a lot of relevant material, would be unable to make any meaningful interpretations from passages like these. This, I felt was necessary to eliminate various, very specific references to cultural or historical happenings found in several places in the Psalms. This would thereby increase the ambiguity of the Psalms—make them more general—and thus make them more widely applicable, and more useful in the here and now. I feel that the Psalms, so edited as I have done, have become more than ever before, now-songs for the now-Christians experiencing now-problems.

And so in the implementation of this principle of ambiguity, I set aside each reference to Jewish history and to geographical location. Animal sacrifices did not seem to be in line with the purpose of the work, nor did references to slaves. Statements reflecting sex-role attitudes of a paternal society I felt might turn some aside from their devotional quest, while a lack of their inclusion would not be disturbing, so these kinds of statements were eliminated or modified to remove the strongly paternal element. There were a few notable exceptions to these minor guiding principles. For example, in Psalm 23 the ancient pastoral symbolism had to be retained in order for the psalm to have any meaning at all.

These, then, were the major and minor principles of inclusion I found myself using as I created the collection of passages which became *Silver in the Psalms*. After using my intellect to analyze the principles of inclusion I had used, I turned to the work of solidifying the collection I had produced and putting it into its final form. Again, since I had been guided by my feeling as I selected the passages for inclusion in the work, I felt that the collection I had produced needed some extra attention. Since feelings are notoriously changeable and unstable, I felt I had better reread all the Psalms, noting what I had included and excluded, in order to see if reading them on a different occasion, perhaps with a slight reorganization of my emotional state, might make any difference. I found that there was little change. I did add a verse, or a part of a verse, here and there, but the collection remained substantially the same—a fact which gave me confidence that the work represented a fairly consistent approach.

I have reproduced the text of the Psalms almost exactly as it appears in *The Living Bible* (Wheaton, Illinois: Tyndale House Publishers, 1971) in all of the psalms except seventeen particular psalms. For these seventeen psalms I used *The King James Version*. My reasoning was this—my primary purpose was communication, and I personally feel that *The Living Bible* excels in clarity, even if it does sacrifice some beauty. But the literary beauty of *The King James Version* is difficult to match; it remains unparalleled in literature, even if it does sacrifice some in clarity of communication. Now, feelings get tied up with familiarity. So, if we are familiar with something, and feel good about it, and then someone comes along and changes the arrangement of the thing we feel good about—although the change may improve several important aspects of it—we nevertheless have a tendency to reject the change. We may reject the change for fear we will lose the positive feelings we have for the familiar passage. This, I feel, accounts for much of the resistance to new versions of the Bible, notwithstanding the many "logical arguments"against a new version.

At any rate, it is important to give respect to these kinds of feelings people have. There are certain psalms which are so familiar to us all, and so widely-known and memorized, that to change them—in almost any way—would be destructive to the feelings of many people. This kind of result would be exactly opposite to the effect I wished to produce. Thus, on the basis of *feeling* again, I made a decision to retain most of the most popular psalms pretty much in their original *King James Version* form. Of course, the decision was a personal one and, thus, somewhat arbitrary. All will not agree with my choices, but that is to be expected with working in the realm of feeling. The psalms presented in the *King James Version* are 1, 8, 19, 21, 23, 24, 27, 40, 46, 51, 90, 91,

100, 103, 118, 121, and 139.

I decided to number each of the Psalms as a whole and to number each of the verses retained from the traditional text. I felt it was very important to help the reader retain the ability to identify particularly meaningful passages and to return to them at will.

The nature of the Psalms is such that, while a general dominant theme might be identified in many of the Psalms, the content of each psalm is very mixed, often making it difficult to identify a single theme. Very often there are several quite different themes in one psalm. Because of the selective work I did in constructing *Silver in the Psalms,* the Psalms in my collection are now more constant with respect to the number and kind of themes remaining in each psalm. But the problem still exists because of the great diversity of subject matter contained in the Psalms.

I have then tried to reduce the problem of multiple themes a little further by subdividing the Psalms according to the major theme I saw to be dominant in a given passage. This has permitted an additional use of the Psalms, as I will elaborate in Part Three. In the task of subdividing, I found little trouble except with Psalm 119. This unusually long psalm had so many themes, many of them recurring several times, that I found it impractical to subdivide. Thus it is referred to in the classification system found in the Appendix, in several categories.

In Part Three, I have suggested several ways to make use of this collection of psalms in devotional Bible study. Part Two is the heart of the work, for it is the "silver" itself. It is vitally a part of me, as I have said. But I want to emphasize one more time that there is much to be learned from the parts of the Scripture not included in my devotional version, and I would encourage the reading of these parts, also. My purpose has not been to decrease the reading of any part of the Psalms, but to enhance its effective use.

PART TWO

The Silver

PSALM 1 (KJV)

(a)   1 Blessed is the [person] who walketh not in the counsel of the ungodly, nor standeth in the way of sinner, nor sitteth in the seat of the scornful. 2 But his delight is in the law of the Lord, and in his law doth he meditate day and night.

(b)   3 And he shall be like a tree planted by the rivers of water, that bringeth forth his fruit in his season, his leaf also shall not wither; and whatsoever he doeth shall prosper. 6 For the Lord knoweth the way of the righteous.

PSALM 2

(a)   6 The Lord declares, "This is the king of my choice." . . . 7 His chosen one replies, "I will reveal the everlasting purposes of God, for the Lord has said to me, 'You are my Son. This is your Coronation Day. Today, I am giving you your glory.' "

(b)   11 Serve the Lord with reverent fear; and rejoice with trembling. 12 Fall down before his Son. . . . Oh, the joys of those who put their trust in him!

PSALM 3

(a)   3 Lord, you are my shield, my glory, and my only hope. You alone can lift my head, now bowed in

31

shame. 4 I cried out to the Lord, and he heard me.
. . . 5 Then I lay down and slept in peace and woke
up safely, for the Lord was watching over me.

(b)   7 I will cry to him, "Arise, O Lord! Save me, O my
God!" 8 Salvation comes from God. What joys he
gives to all his people.

PSALM 4

(a)   1 O God . . . you have always cared for me in my
distress; now hear me as I call again. Have mercy on
me. Hear my prayer. 3 Mark this well: The Lord has
set apart the redeemed for himself. Therefore he will
listen to me and answer when I call to him.

(b)   4 Stand before the Lord in awe, and do not sin
against him. Lie quietly upon your bed in silent meditation. 5 Put your trust in the Lord, and offer him
pleasing sacrifices

(c)   6 O Lord, by letting the light of your face shine
down upon us. 8 I will lie down in peace and sleep,
for though I am alone, O Lord, you will keep me safe.

PSALM 5

(a)   1 O Lord, hear me praying; listen to my plea, O God
my king, for I will never pray to anyone but you.
3 Each morning I will look to you and lay my requests before you, praying earnestly.

(b)   7 I will come into your Temple protected by your
mercy and your love; I will worship you with deepest
awe. 8 Lord, lead me as you promised me you would
. . . Tell me clearly what to do, which way to turn.

(c)   11 Make everyone rejoice who puts his trust in you.
Keep them shouting for joy because you are defending
them. Fill all who love you with your happiness.
12 For you bless the godly person, O Lord; you protect
him with your shield of love.

PSALM 6

(a)   2 Pity me, O Lord, for I am weak. Heal me, for my body is sick, 3 and I am upset and disturbed. My mind is filled with apprehension and with gloom. Oh, restore me soon. 4 Come, O Lord, and make me well. In your kindness save me.

(b)   6 I am worn out with pain; every night my pillow is wet with tears. 7 My eyes are growing old and dim. . . . 8 The Lord has heard my weeping and my pleading. He will answer all my prayers.

PSALM 7

(a)   1 I am depending on you, O Lord my God, to save me . . . . 9 Bless all who truly worship God; for you, the righteous God, look deep within the hearts of men and examine all their motives and their thoughts.

(b)   10 God is my shield; he will defend me. He saves those whose hearts and lives are true and right. 11 God is a judge who is perfectly fair.

(c)   17 Oh, how grateful and thankful I am to the Lord because he is so good. I will sing praise to the name of the Lord who is above all lords.

PSALM 8 (KJV)

(a)   1 O Lord, our Lord, how excellent is thy name in all the earth! who hast set thy glory above the heavens.
3 When I consider thy heavens, the work of thy fingers, the moon and the stars, which thou hast ordained;
4 What is man, that thou art mindful of him? and the son of man, that thou visitest him?

(b)   5 For thou hast made him a little lower than the angels, and hast crowned him with glory and honour.
6 Thou madest him to have dominion over the works of thy hands; thou hast put all things under his feet:
9 O Lord our Lord, how excellent is thy name in all

the earth!

PSALM 9

(a)   1 O Lord, I will praise you with all my heart, and tell everyone about the marvelous things you do. 2 I will be glad, yes, filled with joy because of you. I will sing your praises, O Lord God. . . .

(b)   7,8 The Lord lives on forever; he sits upon his throne to judge justly the nations of the world. 9 All who are oppressed may come to him. He is a refuge for them in their time of trouble. 10 All those who know your mercy, Lord, will count on you for help. For you have never yet forsaken those who trust in you.

(c)   11 Oh, sing out your praises to the God who lives. . . . Tell the world about his unforgettable deeds. 12 He . . . has an open ear to those who cry to him for justice. He does not ignore the prayers of people in trouble when they call upon him for help.

(d)   13 And now, O Lord, have mercy on me; see how I suffer. . . . 14 Save me, so that I can praise you publicly before all the people . . . and rejoice that you have rescued me. The needs of the needy shall not be ignored . . . the hopes of the poor shall not . . . be crushed.

PSALM 10

14 O Lord, the poor man trusts himself to you; you are known as the helper of the helpless. 16 The Lord is King forever and forever. . . . 17 Lord, you know the hopes of humble people. Surely you will hear their cries and comfort their hearts by helping them. 18 You will be with the orphans and all who are oppressed.

PSALM 11

4 The Lord is still in his holy temple; he still rules

. . . He closely watches everything that happens here on earth. 7 For God is good, and he loves goodness; the godly shall see his face.

PSALM 12

(a) 1 Lord! Help! . . . 5 The Lord replies, "I will arise and defend the oppressed, the poor, the needy. I will rescue them as they have longed for me to do.

(b) 6 The Lord's promise is sure. He speaks no careless word; all he says is purest truth, like silver seven times refined. 7 O Lord, we know that you will forever preserve your own.

PSALM 13

3 O Lord my God; give me light in my darkness. . . . 5 I will always trust in you and in your mercy and shall rejoice in your salvation. 6 I will sing to the Lord because he has blessed me so richly.

PSALM 14

(a) 1 That man is foolish who says to himself, "There is no God!" 2 The Lord looks . . . on all mankind to see if there are any who are wise, who want to please God.

(b) 5 God is with those who love him. 6 He is the refuge of the poor and humble. . . . 7 Oh, that the time of their rescue were already here, that God would come . . . now to save his people. What gladness . . . !

PSALM 15

1 Lord, who may go and find refuge and shelter? . . . Anyone who leads a blameless life and is truly sincere. 3 Anyone who refuses to slander others,

does not listen to gossip, never harms his neighbor,
4 . . . commends the faithful followers of the Lord,
keeps a promise . . . 5 such a man shall stand firm
forever.

PSALM 16

(a)   1 Save me, O God, . . . I have come to you for
refuge. 2 I said to him, "You are my Lord; I have no
other help but yours." 3 I want the company of the
godly men and women in the land; they are the true
nobility.

(b)   5 The Lord himself is my inheritance, my prize.
He is my food and drink, my highest joy! He guards
all that is mine. 6 He sees that I am given pleasant
brooks and meadows. . . . What a wonderful inheritance! 7 I will bless the Lord who counsels me; he
gives me wisdom in the night. He tells me what to do.
8 I am always thinking of the Lord; and because he
is so near, I never need to stumble or to fall. 9 Heart,
body, and soul are filled with joy.

(c)   10 For you will not leave me among the dead.
11 You have let me experience the joys of life and the
exquisite pleasures of your own eternal presence.

PSALM 17

(a)   1 I am pleading for your help, O Lord; . . .
I know you will answer me, O God! Yes, listen as I
pray. 7 Show me your strong love in wonderful
ways, O Savior of all those seeking your help . . .
8 Protect me . . . hide me in the shadow of your
wings. . . . 13 Lord, arise and stand against them.

(b)   15 My contentment is not in wealth but in seeing
you and knowing all is well between us. And when
I awake in heaven, I will be fully satisfied, for I will
see you face to face.

(a)　　1 Lord, how I love you! For you have done such
tremendous things for me. 2 The Lord is my fort
where I can enter and be safe; no one can follow me.
. . . He is a rugged mountain where I hide; he is my
Savior, a rock where none can reach me, and a tower
of safety. He is my shield. 3 All I need to do is cry
to him—oh, praise the Lord—and I am saved.

(b)　　6 In my distress I screamed to the Lord for his help.
And he heard me . . . my cry reached his ears. 16 He
reached . . . and took me and drew me out of my
great trials. He rescued me from deep waters. 17 He
delivered me from my strong enemy. . . . 18 On the
day when I was weakest, they attacked. But the Lord
held me steady. 19 He led me to a place of safety.
. . .

(c)　　24 The Lord has paid me with his blessings. . . .
He watches my every step. 25 Lord, how merciful
you are! 26 You give blessings. . . . 27 You deliver the humble. . . . 28 You have turned on my
light! The Lord my God has made my darkness turn
to light. 30 What a God he is! How perfect in every
way! All his promises prove true. He is a shield for
everyone who hides behind him. 31 For who is God
except our Lord? Who but he is as a rock? He fills
me with strength and protects me wherever I go.
33 He leads me safely along . . . 34 and gives me
strength.

(d)　　35 You have given me your salvation as my shield.
Your right hand, O Lord, supports me; your gentle-
ness has made me great. 36 You have made wide steps
beneath my feet so that I need never slip. 46 God is
alive! Praise him who is the great rock of protection.
48 He rescues me. . . . 49 For this, O Lord, I will
praise you. . . . 50 You have been loving and kind

to me and will be. . . .

PSALM 19 (KJV)

(a)   1 The heavens declare the glory of God and the firmament sheweth his handywork. 2 Day unto day uttereth speech . . . 3 There is no speech nor language where their voice is not heard. 4 Their line is gone out through all the earth, and their words to the end of the world.

(b)   7 The law of the Lord is perfect, converting the soul: the testimony of the Lord is sure, making wise the simple. 8 The statues of the Lord are right, rejoicing the heart: the commandment of the Lord is pure, enlightening the eyes. 9 The fear of the Lord is clean, enduring forever: the judgements of the Lord are true and righteous altogether. 10 More to be desired are they than gold, yea, than much fine gold: sweeter also than honey. . . . 11 Moreover, by them is thy servant warned warned: . . . in keeping of them there is great reward.

(c)   12 Who can understand his errors? cleanse thou me from secret faults. 13 Keep back thy servant also from presumptuous sins; let them not have dominion over me: then shall I be upright, . . . and innocent. 14 Let the words of my mouth, and the meditation of my heart, be acceptable in thy sight, O Lord, my strength and my redeemer.

PSALM 20

(a)   1 In your day of trouble, may the Lord be with you! May . . . God . . . keep you from all harm. 2 May he send you aid. . . . 4 May he grant you your heart's desire and fulfill all your plans. 5 May there be shouts of joy when we hear the news of your victory, flags flying with praise to God for all that he has done for you.

(c)   May he answer all your prayers! 6 He hears . . . and sends great victories. 9 Give victory . . . O Lord;

oh hear our prayer.

PSALM 21 (KJV)

(a)   1 [We] shall rejoice in thy strength, O Lord; and in thy salvation how greatly shall [we] rejoice! 2 Thou hast given [us] our heart's desire, and hast not withholden the request of [our] lips. 3 [You have welcomed us.] . . . 6 Thou hast made [us] blessed for ever . . . and made [us] exceeding glad with thy countenance. 7 [We trust] in the Lord, and through the mercy of the most High [we] shall not be moved. 13 Be thou exalted, Lord, in thine own strength.

(b)   We will sing and praise thy power.

PSALM 22

(a)   3,4 You are holy; The praises of our fathers surrounded your throne; they trusted you and you delivered them. 5 You heard their cries for help and saved them; they were never disappointed when they sought your aid. 9, 10, 11 Lord, how you have helped me before! . . . I have depended upon you since birth; you have always been my God.

(b)   Don't leave me now, for my trouble is near and no one else can possibly help. 14 My strength has drained away like water. . . . My heart melts like wax; my strength has dried up. . . . 19 O Lord don't stay away. O God my Strength, hurry to my aid. 20 Rescue me. . . .

(c)   21 God will answer me and rescue me. 22 I will praise you to all my brothers; I will stand up before the congregation and testify of the wonderful things you have done. 23 "Praise the Lord, each one of you who fears him," I will say. "Each of you must fear and reverence his name. Let all Israel sing his praises,

24 for he has not despised my cries of deep despair; he has not turned and walked away. When I cried to him, he heard and came." 25 Yes, I will stand and praise him before all the people. I will publicly fulfill my vows in the presence of all who reverence your name.

(d)   26 The poor shall eat and be satisfied; all who seek the Lord shall find him and shall praise his name. Their hearts shall rejoice with everlasting joy. 27 The whole earth shall see it and return to the Lord; the people of every nation shall worship him.

(e)   28 For the Lord is King and rules the nations. 29 Both the proud and the humble together, all who are mortal—born to die—shall worship him. 30 Our children too shall serve him, for they shall hear from us about the wonders of the Lord; 31 Generations yet unborn shall hear of all the miracles he did for us.

PSALM 23 (KJV)

1 The Lord is my shepherd; I shall not want. 2 He maketh me to lie down in green pastures; he leadeth me beside the still waters; he restoreth my soul. He leadeth me in the paths of righteousness for his name's sake. 4 Yea, though I walk through the valley of the shadow of death, I will fear no evil, for thou art with me. Thy rod and thy staff they comfort me. 5 Thou preparest a table before me. . . . thou anointest my head with oil; my cup runneth over. 6 Surely goodness and mercy shall follow me all the days of my life, and I will dwell in the house of the Lord for ever.

PSALM 24 (KJV)

(a)   1 The earth is the Lord's and the fulness thereof, the world and they that dwell therein. 2 For he hath founded it upon the seas, and established it. . . .

3 who shall ascend into the hill of the Lord? or who
shall stand in his holy place? 4 He that hath clean
hands, and a pure heart; who hath not lifted up his
soul unto vanity. . . . 5 He shall receive the blessing
from the Lord, and righteousness from the God of his
salvation. 6 This is the generation of them that seek him.
. . .

(b)   7 Lift up your heads, O ye gates; and be ye lift up,
ye everlasting doors; and the King of glory shall come
in. 8 Who is this king of glory? The Lord, strong and
mighty. . . . 9 Lift up your heads, O ye gates, even
lift them up, ye everlasting doors; and the King of
glory shall come in. 10 Who is this King of glory?
The Lord . . . is the King of glory.

PSALM 25

(a)   1 To you, O Lord, I pray. 2 Don't fail me, Lord,
for I am trusting in you. . . . 3 None who have
faith in God will ever be disgraced for trusting him.
. . . 4 Show me the path where I should go, O Lord;
point out the right road for me to walk. 5 Lead me;
teach me; for you are the God who gives me salvation.
I have no hope except in you. 6, 7 O Lord! Look at
me through eyes of mercy and forgiveness, through
eyes of everlasting love and kindness. 8 The Lord is
good and glad to teach the proper path to all who go
astray; 9 he will teach the ways that are right and best
to those who humbly turn to him. 10 And when we
obey him, every path he guides us on is fragrant with
his lovingkindness and his truth.

(b)   11 But Lord, my sins! How many they are. Oh,
pardon them for the honor of your name.

(c)   12 Where is the man who fears the Lord? God
will teach him how to choose the best. 13 He shall
live within God's circle of blessing, and his children
shall inherit the earth. 14 Friendship with God is

41

reserved for those who reverence him. With them alone he shares the secrets of his promises.

(d)   15 My eyes are ever looking to the Lord for help, for he alone can rescue me. 16 Come, Lord, and show me your mercy, for I am helpless, overwhelmed, in deep distress; 17 my problems go from bad to worse. Oh, save me from them all! 18 See my sorrows; feel my pain; forgive my sins. 21 Assign me Godliness and Integrity as my bodyguards, for I am trusting you to protect me.

PSALM 26

(a)   1 I have tried to keep your laws and have trusted you . . . 3 I have taken your lovingkindness and your truth as my ideals. 6 I . . . come before your altar, singing a song of thanksgiving. . . .

(b)   8 Lord, I love your home. . . . 11 I try to walk a straight and narrow path of doing what is right. . . . 12 I publicly praise the Lord for keeping me from slipping and falling.

PSALM 27 (KJV)

(a)   1 The Lord is my light and salvation; whom shall I fear? the Lord is the strength of my life; of whom shall I be afraid? . . . 3 In this will I be confident. 4 One thing have I desired of the Lord, that I will seek after; that I may dwell in the house of the Lord all the days of my life, to behold the beauty of the Lord, and to meditate in his [Church]. 5 In the time of trouble he shall hide me in his pavilion, in the secret of his tabernacle shall he hide me; he shall set me upon a rock. . . . 6 Therefore will I offer . . . sacrifices of joy; I will sing, yea, I will sing praises unto the Lord.

(b)   7 Hear, O Lord, when I cry with my voice: have mercy also upon me, and answer me. 8 When thou saidst, Seek ye my face; my heart said unto thee,

Thy face, Lord, will I seek. . . . 9 Thou has been my help. . . . 10 If my father and my mother forsake me then the Lord will take me up. 11 Teach me thy way, O Lord, and lead me in a plain path. . . . I had fainted, unless I had believed to see the goodness of the Lord in the land of the living.

(c)   14 Wait on the Lord; be of good courage, and he shall strengthen thine heart: wait, I say, on the Lord.

PSALM 28

(a)   1 I plead with you to help me Lord, for you are my Rock of safety. . . . 2 Lord, I lift my hands to heaven and implore your help. Oh, listen to my cry.

(b)   6 Oh, praise the Lord, for he has listened to my pleadings! 7 He is my strength, my shield from every danger. I trusted in him, and he helped me. Joy rises in my heart until I burst out in songs of praise to him.

PSALM 29

      1 Praise the Lord . . . praise his glory and his strength. 2 Praise him for his majestic glory, the glory of his name. . . . 9 In his temple all are praising, "Glory, glory to the Lord." 10 He continues to unveil his power. 11 He will give his people strength. He will bless them with peace.

PSALM 30

(a)   1 I will praise you, Lord, for you have saved me. . . . 2 O Lord my God, I pleaded with you, and you gave me my health. . . . 4 Oh, sing to him you saints of his; give thanks to his holy name. 5 . . . His favor lasts for life! Weeping may go on all night, but in the morning there is joy.

(b)   6, 7 In my prosperity I said, "This is forever; nothing can stop me now! The Lord has shown me his favor. He

43

has made me as steady as a mountain." . . . Suddenly
my courage was gone; I was terrified and panic-stricken.
8 I cried to you, O Lord; oh, how I pled: . . .
10 "Hear me, Lord; oh have pity and help me."

(c)   Then he turned my sorrow into joy! . . . 12 O Lord
my God, I will keep on thanking you forever!

PSALM 31

(a)   1 Lord, I trust in you alone. . . . Rescue me because you are the God who always does what is right.
2 Answer quickly when I cry to you; bend low and
hear my whispered plea. Be for me a great Rock of
safety. 3 Yes, you are my Rock. . . . 4 You alone
are strong enough. 5,6 Into your hand I commit my
spirit.

(b)   You have rescued me, O God who keeps his promises.
I worship only you. . . . 7 I am radiant with joy because of your mercy, for you have listened to my
troubles and have seen the crisis in my soul. 8 You
have given me open ground in which to maneuver.

(c)   9 O Lord, have mercy on me. . . . 14, 15 I . . .
trust you, O Lord. I said, "You alone are my God;
my times are in your hands. Rescue me. . . . 16 Let
your favor shine again upon your servant; save me just
because you are so kind! 19 Oh, how great is your
goodness to those who publicly declare that you will
rescue them. For you have stored up great blessings
for those who trust and reverence you. 20 Hide your
loved ones in the shelter of your presence, safe beneath
your hand, safe. . . .

(d)   21 Blessed is the Lord, for he has shown me that his
never-failing love protects me. . . . 22 You listened
to my plea and answered me. 23 Oh, love the Lord,
all of you who are his people; for the Lord protects
those who are loyal to him. . . . 24 So cheer up!

Take courage if you are depending on the Lord.

PSALM 32

(a)   1, 2 What happiness for those who guilt has been forgiven! What joys when sins are covered over! What relief for those who have confessed their sins and God
has cleared their record. 3 There was a time when I
wouldn't admit what a sinner I was. But my dishon-
esty made me miserable and filled my days with frustration. 4 All day and all night your hand was heavy
upon me. My strength evaporated like water on a sunny
day, 5 until I finally admitted all of my sins to you
and stopped trying to hide them. I said to myself,
"I will confess them to the Lord." And you forgave
me! All my guilt is gone! 6 Now I say that each be-
liever should confess his sins to God when he is aware
of them, while there is time to be forgiven. Judgment
will not touch him if he does.

(b)   7 You are my hiding place from every storm of life;
You even keep me from getting into trouble! You surround me with songs of victory. 8 I will instruct you
(says the Lord) and guide you along the best pathway
for your life; I will advise you and watch your progress.

(c)   10 Abiding love surrounds those who trust in the
Lord. 11 So rejoice in him, all those who are his,
and shout for joy, all those who try to obey him.

PSALM 33

(a)   1 Let all the joys of the godly well up in praise to
the Lord, for it is right to praise him. 2 Play joyous
melodies of praise. . . . 3 Compose new songs of
praise . . . sing joyfully. 4 For all God's words are
right, and everything he does is worthy of our trust.
5 He loves whatever is just and good; the earth is
filled with his tender love.

(b)   8 Let everyone in all the world—men, women, and
        children—fear the Lord and stand in awe of him.
        9 For when he but spoke, the world began! It appeared
        at his command! 11 His own plan stands forever. His
        intentions are the same for every generation. 12 Bles-
        sed is the nation whose God is the Lord. . . .

(c)   18 The eyes of the Lord are watching over those
        who fear him, who rely upon his steady love. 20 We
        depend upon the Lord alone to save us. Only he can
        help us; he protects us like a shield. 21 No wonder
        we are happy in the Lord! For we are trusting him.
        We trust his holy name. 22 Yes, Lord, let your con-
        stant love surround us, for our hopes are in you alone.

PSALM 34

(a)   1 I will praise the Lord no matter what happens.
        I will constantly speak of his glories and grace. 2 I
        will boast of all his kindness to me. Let all who are
        discouraged take heart. 3 Let us praise the Lord to-
        gether, and exalt his name. 4 For I cried to him and
        he answered me! He freed me from all my fears.

(b)   5 Others too were radiant at what he did for them.
        Theirs was no downcast look of rejection! 6 This
        poor man cried out to the Lord—and the Lord heard him
        and saved him out of his troubles. 8 Oh, put God to
        the test and see how kind he is! See for yourself the
        way his mercies shower down on all who trust in him.

(c)   9 If you belong to the Lord, reverence him; for
        everyone who does this has everything he needs.
        10 Those of us who reverence the Lord will never lack
        any good thing. 11 Sons and daughters, come and lis-
        ten and let me teach you the importance of trusting and
        fearing the Lord. 14 Turn from all known sin and
        spend your time in doing good. Try to live in peace
        with everyone; work hard at it. 15 For the eyes of

46

the Lord are intently watching all who live good lives, and he gives attention when they cry to him.

(d)   17 The Lord hears the good man when he calls to him for help, and saves him out of all his troubles. 18 The Lord is close to those whose hearts are breaking; he rescues those who are humbly sorry for their sins.

(e)   19 The good man does not escape all troubles—he has them too. But the Lord helps him in each and every one. 22 He will redeem them; but everyone who takes refuge in him will be freely pardoned.

PSALM 35

(a)   9 I will rejoice in the Lord. He shall rescue me! 10 From the bottom of my heart praise rises to him. Where is his equal in all of heaven and earth? Who else protects the weak and helpless from the strong, and the poor and needy from those who would rob them? 18 Save me, and

(b)   I will thank you publicly before the entire congregation, before the largest crowd I can find. 27 "Great is the Lord who enjoys helping his child!" 28 I will tell everyone how great and good you are; I will praise you all day long.

PSALM 36

     5 Your steadfast love, O Lord, is as great as all the heavens. Your faithfulness reaches beyond the clouds. . . . 6 Your justice is as solid as God's mountains. Your decisions are as full of wisdom as the oceans are with water. You are concerned for men and animals alike. 7 How precious is your constant love, O God! All humanity takes refuge in the shadow of your wings. 8 You feed them with blessings from your own table and let them drink from your rivers of delight. 9 For you are the Fountain of life; our light is from your Light. 10 Pour out your unfailing love on those who

know you! Never stop giving your salvation to those who long to do your will.

PSALM 37

(a)   1 Never envy the wicked. 3 Trust in the Lord. . . . Be kind and good to others; then you will live safely here in the land and prosper, feeding in safety. 4 Be delighted with the Lord. Then he will give you all your heart's desires. 5 Commit everything you do to the Lord. Trust him to help you do it and he will. 6 Your innocence will be clear to everyone. He will vindicate you with the blazing light of justice shining down as from the noonday sun.

(b)   7 Rest in the Lord; wait patiently for him to act. . . . 8 Don't fret and worry—it only leads to harm. 9 Those who trust the Lord shall be given every blessing. 11 All who humble themselves before the Lord shall be given every blessing, and shall have wonderful peace. 17 The Lord takes care of those he has forgiven.

(c)   18 Day by day the Lord observes the good deeds done by godly men, and gives them eternal rewards. 19 He cares for them when times are hard; even in famine, they will have enough. 21 The good man returns what he owes with some extra besides. 22 Those blessed by the Lord shall inherit the earth. . . .

(d)   23 The steps of good persons are directed by the Lord. He delights in each step they take. 24 If they fall it isn't fatal, for the Lord holds them with his hand. 25 I have been young and now am old. And in all my years I have never seen the Lord forsake a person who loves him. . . .

(e)   26 The godly are able to be generous with their gifts and loans to others, and their children usually are a blessing. 28 The Lord loves justice and fairness; he will

48

never abandon his people. They will be kept safe forever. . . . 29 The godly shall be firmly planted in
the land, and live there forever. 30, 31 The godly person is a good counselor because he is just and fair and
knows right from wrong.

(f)   34 Don't be impatient for the Lord to act! Keep
traveling steadily along his pathway and in due season
he will honor you with every blessing. . . . 37 The
good—the upright, the person of peace—he has a wonderful future ahead of him. For him there is a happy
ending. 39 The Lord saves the godly. He is their salvation and their refuge when trouble comes. Because
they trust in him, he helps them.

PSALM 38

15 I am waiting for you, O Lord my God. Come and
protect me. 17 How constantly I find myself upon the
verge of sin; this source of sorrow always stares me in
the face. 18 I confess my sins; I am sorry for what I
have done. 21 Don't leave me, Lord; don't go away!
22 Come quickly! Help me, O my Savior.

PSALM 39

1 I said to myself, I'm going to quit complaining!
I'll keep quiet. . . . 2,3 But as I stood there silently
the turmoil within me grew to the bursting point. The
more I mused, the hotter the fires inside. Then at last
I spoke and pled with God: 4 "Lord, help me to realize how brief my time on earth will be. Help me to
know that I am here but for a moment more. 5 My
life is no longer than my hand! My whole lifetime
is but a moment to you. . . . 7 And so, Lord, my
only hope is in you. 9 Lord, I am speechless before
you. I will not open my mouth to speak one word of
complaint. . . . 12 Hear my prayer, O Lord; listen

to my cry! . . . For I am your guest. I am a traveler passing through the earth. . . . 13 Let me be filled with happiness again.

PSALM 40 (KJV)

(a) 1 I waited patiently for the Lord; and he inclined unto me, and heard my cry. 2 He brought me up also out of an horrible pit, out of the miry clay, and set my feet upon a rock, and established my goings.

(b) 3 He hath put a new song in my mouth, even praise unto our God: many shall see it [and stand in awe], and shall trust in the Lord. 4 Blessed is that [person] who maketh the Lord his trust. . . .

(c) 5 Many, O Lord my God, are thy wonderful works which thou hast done, and thy thoughts which are to us-ward: they cannot be reckoned up in order unto thee: if I would declare and speak of them, they are more than can be numbered.

(d) 6 Sacrifice and offering thou didst not desire; mine ears hast thou opened. . . . 8 I delight to do thy will, O my God; yea, thy law is within my heart. 9 I have preached righteousness in the great congreagation; lo, I have not refrained my lips, O Lord, thou knowest.

(e) 11 Withhold not thou thy tender mercies from me, O Lord; let thy lovingkindness and thy truth continually preserve me. 12 Innumerable evils have compassed me about: mine iniquities have taken hold upon me, so that I am not able to look up; they are more than the hairs of mine head: therefore my heart faileth me.

13 Be pleased, O Lord, to deliver me: O Lord, make haste to help me. 16. Let all those that seek thee rejoice and be glad in thee: let such as love thy salvation say continually, The Lord be magnified. 17 I am poor and needy; yet the Lord thinketh upon me: thou art my help and my deliverer.

PSALM 41

1 God blesses those who are kind to the poor. He helps them out of their troubles. 2 He protects them and keeps them. . . . 4 "O Lord," I prayed, "be kind and heal me, for I have confessed my sins." 12 You have preserved me . . . you have admitted me forever to your presence. 13 Bless the Lord, . . . God . . . who exists from everlasting ages past—and on into everlasting eternity ahead. Amen.

PSALM 42

1 As the deer pants for water, so I long for you, O God. 2 I thirst for God, the living God. . . .
4, 5 Take courage my soul! Do you remember those times . . . when you . . . [were] singing with joy, praising the Lord? Why then be downcast? Why be discouraged and sad? Hope in God! I shall yet praise him again. Yes, I shall again praise him for his help.
6 I will meditate upon your kindness. . . . 8 Day by day the Lord also pours out his steadfast love upon me, and through the night I sing his songs and pray to God who gives me life. 11 O my soul, don't be discouraged. Don't be upset. Expect God to act! For I know that I shall again have plenty of reason to praise him for all that he will do. He is my help! He is my God!

PSALM 43

1 O God, . . . 2 you are . . . my only place of refuge. . . . 3 Oh, send out your light and your truth —let them lead me. 4 I will go to . . . God my exceeding joy, and praise him. . . . O God—my God!
5 O my soul, why be so gloomy and discouraged? Trust in God! I shall again praise him for his wondrous help; he will make me smile again, for he is my God!

PSALM 44

1 O God, we have heard of the glorious miracles you did in the days of long ago. . . . 4 You are my King and my God. Decree victories for your people. 7 Only you can give us the victory. . . . 8 My constant boast is God. I can never thank you enough! . . . 26 O Lord . . . come and help us. Save us by your constant love.

PSALM 45

1 My heart is overflowing with a beautiful thought! I will write a lovely poem to the King, for I am as full of words as the speediest writer pouring out his story. 2 You are the fairest of all; your words are filled with grace: God himself is blessing you forever. 3 So glorious, so majestic! 4 and in your majesty go on to victory, defending truth, humility, and justice. Go forth to awe-inspiring deeds! . . . 6 Your throne, O God, endures forever. justice is your royal scepter. 7 You love what is good. . . . Therefore God, your God, has given you more gladness. . . . 17 "I will cause your name to be honored in all generations."

PSALM 46 (KJV)

1 God is our refuge and strength, a very present help in trouble. 2 Therefore will not we fear, though the earth be removed, and though the mountains be carried into the midst of the sea; though the waters thereof roar and be troubled; though the mountains shake with the swellings thereof. . . . 4 There is a river, the streams whereof shall make glad the city of God. . . . 5 God is there. . . . 7 God . . . is our refuge. . . . 10 Be still and know that I am God; I will be exalted . . . in the earth! 11 The Lord is with us; God . . . is our refuge.

PSALM 47

1 Come, everyone, and clap for joy! Shout triumphant praises to the Lord! 2 For the Lord . . . God . . . is awesome beyond words; he is the great King of all the earth. 3, 4 He . . . will personally select his choicest blessings . . . —the very best for those he loves. 5 God has ascended with a mighty shout. . . . 6, 7 Sing out your praises to our God, our King. Yes, sing your highest praises to our King, the King of all the earth. Sing thoughtful praises! 8 He reigns. . . . 9 He is highly honored everywhere.

PSALM 48

1 How great is the Lord! How much we should praise him. He lives. . . . 2 What a glorious sight! . . . High . . . for all to see—joy of all the earth . . . the great King. 8 We have heard of . . . the city of our God, the Commander. . . . And now we see it for ourselves! . . . 9 Lord, here among your Temple we meditate upon your kindness and your love. 10 Your name is known throughout the earth, O God. You are praised everywhere for the salvation you have scattered throughout the world. . . . 14 This great God is our God forever and ever. He will be our guide until we die.

PSALM 49

(a) 1,2, Listen, everyone! High and low, rich and poor, all around the world—listen to my words. . . . 5 There is no need to fear when times of trouble come. . . . 8, 9 A soul is far too precious to be ransomed by mere earthly wealth. Thee is not enough of it in all the earth to buy eternal life for just one soul. . . .

(b) 10 Rich man! Proud man! Wise man! You must die like all the rest! . . . 14 Death is the shepherd of all mankind. . . . 15 But . . . God will redeem my soul

from the power of death, for he will receive me. 16 So
do not be dismayed.

PSALM 50

1 The mighty God, the Lord, has summoned all mankind from east to west! 2 God's glory-light shines. . .
4 To heaven and earth he shouts, 5 "Gather together
my own people who . . . have promised to obey me."
6 God will judge them with complete fairness, for all
heavens declare that he is just. 7 O my people, listen!
For I am your God. Listen! . . . 9 It isn't sacrificial
bullocks and goats that I really want from you.
10, 11 For all . . . are mine! 12 All the world is
mine, and everything in it. 13 No, I don't need your
sacrifices of flesh and blood. 14, 15 What I want from
you is your true thanks; I want your promises fulfilled.
I want you to trust me in your times of trouble, so I
can rescue you, and you can give me glory. . . .
23 True praise is a worthy sacrifice. . . . Those who
walk my paths will receive salvation from the Lord.

PSALM 51 (KJV)

1 Have mercy upon me, O God, according to thy
lovingkindness: according to the multitude of thy
tender mercies, blot out my transgressions. 2 Wash me
thoroughly from mine iniquity, and cleanse me from
my sin. 3 I acknowledge my transgressions, and my
sin is ever before me. 4 Against thee, thee only, have
I sinned, and done evil in thy sight. [You saw it all, and
your sentence against me is just.] . . . 6 Thou de-
sirest truth in the inward parts: and in the hidden part
thou shalt make me to know wisdom. 7 Purge me . . .
and I shall be clean: wash me, and I shall be whiter
than snow. 8 Make me to hear joy and gladness . . .
9 Hide thy face from my sins, and blot out all mine

iniquities. 10 Create in me a clean heart; O God, and renew a right spirit within me. . . . 12 Restore unto me the joy of thy salvation; and uphold me with thy free spirit. 13 Then will I teach transgressors thy ways; and sinners shall be converted unto thee. 14 Deliver me from blood guiltiness, O God, thou God of my salvation: and my tongue shall sing aloud of thy righteousness. 15 O Lord, open thou my lips; and my mouth shall shew forth thy praise. . . . 17 The sacrifices to God are a broken spirit . . . a broken and a contrite heart, O God, thou wilt not despise. 18 Do good in thy good pleasure. . . . 19 Thou shalt be pleased with the sacrifice of righteousness.

PSALM 52

8 I am . . . sheltered . . . protected by the Lord himself. I trust in the mercy of God forever and ever. 9 O Lord, I will praise you forever and ever. . . . And I will wait for your mercies—for everyone knows what a merciful God you are.

PSALM 53

1 Only a fool would say to himself, "There is no God." . . . 2 God looks . . . searching among all mankind to see if there is a single one who does right and really seeks for God. 6 Oh . . . God . . . come . . . now and save Israel! Only when the Lord himself restores them can they ever be really happy again.

PSALM 54

(a)   1 Come with great power, O God, and save me! Defend me with your might! 2 Oh, listen to my prayer.

(b)   4 God is my helper. He is a friend of mine! 5 O God. . . . 6 Gladly . . . will I praise your name, . . . for you are good. God has rescued me from all my trouble.

PSALM 55

(a)   1 Listen to my prayer, O God . . . 2 Hear me, Lord! Listen to me! 6 Oh, for wings like a dove, to fly away and rest! 7 I would fly to far off deserts and stay there. 8 I would flee to some refuge from all this storm. 14 What fellowship we had, what wonderful discussions as we walked together to the Temple of the Lord on holy days.

(b)   16 I will call upon the Lord to save me—and he will. 17 I will pray morning, noon, and night, pleading aloud with God; and he will hear and answer. 18 Though the tide of battle runs strong against me . . . yet he will rescue me. 19 God himself—God from everlasting ages past—will answer. 22 Give your burdens to the Lord. He will carry them. He will not permit the godly to slip or fall. 23 I am trusting you to save me.

PSALM 56

1 Lord, have mercy on me. . . . 3, 4 When I am afraid, I will put my confidence in you. Yes, I will trust the promises of God. And since I am trusting in him, what can mere man do to me? 8 You have seen me tossing and turning through the night. You have collected all my tears and preserved them in your bottle! You have recorded every one in your book. 9 The very day I call for help, the tide . . . turns. . . . This one thing I know: God is for me! 10, 11 I am trusting God—oh, praise his promises! I am not afraid of anything mere man can do to me! Yes, praise his promises. 12 I will surely do what I have promised, Lord, and thank you for your help. 13 For you have saved me from death and my feet from slipping, so that I can walk before the Lord in the land of the living.

PSALM 57

(a)   1 O God, have pity, for I am trusting you! I will hide beneath the shadow of your wings until this storm is past. 2 I will cry to the God of heaven who does such wonders for me. 3 He will send help . . . to save me, because of his love and his faithfulness. He will rescue me. . . . 5 Lord, be exalted above the highest heavens! Show your glory high above the earth.

(b)   7 O God, my heart is quiet and confident. No wonder I can sing your praises!

(c)   8 Rouse yourself, my soul! Arise. . . . . Let us greet the day with song! 9 I will thank you publicly throughout the land. I will sing your praises. . . . 10 Your kindness and love are as vast as the heavens. Your faithfulness is higher than the skies. 11 Yes, be exalted, O God, above the heavens. May your glory shine throughout the earth.

PSALM 58

10 The godly shall rejoice in the triumph of right. . . . 11 Then at last everyone will know that good is rewarded, and that there is a God who judges justly.

PSALM 59

(a)   1 O my God, save me. . . . Protect me. . . . 2 Preserve me. . . . 4 Help me! O God my Strength! I will sing your praises, for you are my place of safety. 10 My God is changeless in his love for me and he will come and help me.

(b)   16 I will sing each morning about your power and mercy. For you have been my place of refuge, a place of safety in the day of my distress. 17 O my Strength to you I sing my praises; for you are my place of safety, my God of mercy.

PSALM 60

2 Lord, heal it now, for it is shaken to the depths.
4, 5 You have given us a banner to rally to; all who
love truth will rally to it. . . . Use your strong right
arm to rescue us. 6, 7 God has promised to help us.
He has vowed it by his holiness! 9, 10 Who will bring
me in triumph . . .? God will! 11 Yes, Lord, help
us. . . . 12 With God's help we shall do mighty
things.

PSALM 61

(a) 1 O God, listen to me! Hear my prayer! 2 For
wherever I am, though far away at the ends of the
earth, I will cry to you for help. When my heart is
faint and overwhelmed, lead me to the mighty, towering
Rock of safety.

(b) 3 You are my refuge. . . . 4 I shall live forever in
your tabernacle; oh, to be safe beneath the shelter of
your wings! 5 You have heard my vows, O God, to
praise you every day, and you have given me the blessings you reserve for those who reverence your name.
7 I shall live before the Lord forever. Oh, send your
lovingkindness and truth to guard and watch over me,
8 and I will praise your name continually, fulfilling my
vow of praising you each day.

PSALM 62

(a) 1 I stand silently before the Lord, waiting for him to
rescue me. For salvation comes from him alone. 2 Yes,
he alone is my Rock, my rescuer, defense. . . . Why
then should I be tense with fear when troubles come?
7 My protection and success come from God alone. He
is my refuge, a Rock where no enemy can reach me.

(b) 8 O my people, trust him all the time. Pour out your
longings before him, for he can help! He is loving and

kind and rewards each of us according to the work we
do for him.

PSALM 63

(a)   1 O God, my God! How I search for you! How I
thirst for you. . . . How I long to find you! 2 How I
wish I could go into your presence to see your strength
and glory, 3 for your love and kindness are better to me
than life itself. How I praise you! 4 I will bless you as
long as I live, lifting up my hands to you in prayer.
5 At last I shall be fully satisfied; I will praise you with
great joy.

(b)   6 I lie awake at night thinking of you— 7 of how
much you have helped me—and how I rejoice through
the night beneath the protecting shadow of your wings.
8 I follow close behind you, protected by your strong
right arm. 11 I will rejoice in God. All who trust in him
exult.

PSALM 64

(a)   1 Lord, listen to my complaint. . . . 7 God himself
will. . . .

(b)   9 Everyone shall stand in awe and confess the greatness of the miracles of God; at last they will realize what
amazing things he does. 10 And the godly shall rejoice
in the Lord, and trust and praise him.

PSALM 65

(a)   1, 2 O God, we wait before you in silent praise. . . .
And because you answer prayer, all mankind will come
to you with their requests. 3 Though sins fill our
hearts, you forgive them all.

(b)   4 How greatly to be envied are those who have
chosen to come and live with you. . . . What joys
await us among all the good things there. 5 O God who

59

saves us. You are the only hope of all mankind throughout the world. . . .

(c)   6 He formed the mountains by his mighty strength. 8 The glorious acts of God shall startle everyone. The dawn and sunset shout for joy! 12 Hillsides blossom with joy. 13 All the world shouts with joy, and sings.

PSALM 66

(a)   1 Sing to the Lord, all the earth! 2 Sing of his glorious name! Tell the world how wonderful he is. 3 How awe-inspiring are your deeds, O God! How great your power! . . . 4 All the earth shall worship you and sing of your glories. 5 Come, see the glorious things God has done. 8 Let everyone bless God and sing his praises, for he holds our lives in his hands. And he holds our feet to the path.

(b)   16 Come and hear, all of you who reverence the Lord, and I will tell you what he did for me: 17 For I cried to him for help, with praises ready on my tongue. 19 He listened! He heard my prayer! He paid attention to it! 20 Blessed be God who didn't turn away when I was praying, and didn't refuse me his kindness and love.

PSALM 67

1 O God, in mercy bless us; let your face beam with joy as you look at us. 2 Send us around the world with the news of your saving power and your eternal plan for all mankind. 3 How everyone throughout the earth will praise the Lord! 4 How glad the nations will be, singing for joy because you are their King and will give true justice to their people! Praise God, O world! May all the peoples of the earth gives thanks to you. 6, 7 God, even our own God, will bless us. And peoples from remotest lands will worship him.

3 May the godly man exult. May he rejoice and be merry. 4 Sing praises to the Lord! Raise your voice in song to him . . . oh, rejoice in his presence. 5 He is a father to the fatherless. . . . 6 He gives families to the lonely and releases prisoners . . . singing with joy! 18 God will live among us here. 19 What a glorious Lord! He who daily bears our burdens also gives us our salvation. He frees us! He rescues us. . . . 22 The Lord says, "Come." . . . 26 Let all the people . . . praise the Lord. . . . 32 Sing to the Lord . . . sing praises to the Lord. 34 Power belongs to God! . . . 35 What awe we feel, kneeling . . . before him. . . . God . . . gives strength and mighty power to his people. Blessed be God.

PSALM 69

(a) 1, 2 Save me, O my God. The floods have risen. Deeper and deeper I sink in the mire; the waters rise around me. 3 I have wept until I am exhausted; my throat is dry and hoarse; my eyes are swollen with weeping. . . . 5 O God, you know so well how stupid I am, and you know all my sins. 6 O God . . . don't let me be a stumbling block to those who trust in you. 9 My zeal for God and his work burns hot within me. . . . 13 I keep right on praying to you, Lord. For now is the time . . . you hear! You are ready with a plentiful supply of love and kindness. Now answer my prayer and rescue me. . . . 14 Pull me out of this mire. Don't let me sink in. Rescue me . . . from these deep waters I am in. 15 Don't let the floods overwhelm me. . . . 16 O Jehovah, answer my prayers, for your lovingkindness is wonderful; your mercy is so plentiful, so tender and so kind. 17 I am in deep trouble. Quick! Come and save me. 18 Come, Lord, and rescue me. Ransom me.

(b)   30 I will praise God with my singing! My thanks will be his praise. 32 The humble shall see their God at work for them. No wonder they will be so glad! All who seek for God shall live in joy. 33 Jehovah hears the cries of his needy ones, and does not look the other way. 14 Praise him. . . . 15 For God will save.

PSALM 70

1 Rescue me, O God! Lord, hurry to my aid! 4 Fill the followers of God with joy. Let those who love your salvation exclaim, "What a wonderful God he is!" 5 I am in deep trouble. Rush to my aid, for only you can help and save me. O Lord, don't delay.

PSALM 71

(a)   1 Lord, you are my refuge! . . . 2 Save me. . . . Rescue me! Listen to my plea and save me. 3 Be to me a great protecting Rock, where I am always welcome, safe from all attacks. 4 Rescue me, O God. . . . 5 You alone are my hope.

(b)   I've trusted you from childhood. 6 Yes, you have been with me from birth and have helped me constantly —no wonder I am always praising you! 8 All day long I'll praise and honor you, O God, for all that you have done for me. 12 O God. . . . Come quickly! Help! 14 I will keep on expecting you to help me. I praise you more and more. 15 I cannot count the times when you have faithfully rescued me from danger. I will tell everyone how good you are, and of your constant, daily care. 16 I walk in the strength of the Lord God. I tell everyone that you alone are just and good. 17 O God, you have helped me from my earliest childhood— and I have constantly testified to others of the wonderful things you do. 19 Your power and goodness, Lord, reach to the highest heavens. You have done such wonderful things. . . . 20 you will bring me back to life again, up from the depths. . . . 21 You will . . . comfort me. 22 I will praise you with music, telling of your faithfulness to all your promises. . . . 23 I will shout and sing your praises for redeeming me. 24 I will talk to others all day long about your justice and your goodness.

PSALM 72

(a)   1 O God, help the King to judge as you would, and help his son to walk in godliness. 2 Help him to give justice to your people. . . .

(b)   4 Help . . . the poor and needy. . . . 5 May the poor and needy revere you constantly. . . . 12 He will take care of the helpless and poor when they cry to him; for they have no one else to defend them. 13 He feels pity for the weak and needy, and will rescue them. 14 He will save them from oppression and from violence, for their lives are precious to him.

(c)   16 Bless us with abundant crops throughout the land. . . . 17 His name will be honored forever; it will continue as the sun; and all will be blessed in him; all nations will praise him. 18 Blessed be . . . God . . . who only does wonderful things! 19 Blessed be his glorious name forever! Let the whole earth be filled with his glory. Amen!

PSALM 73

(a)   1 How good God is to Israel—to those whose hearts are pure. 2 But as for me, I came so close to the edge of the cliff! My feet were slipping and I was almost gone. 3 For I was envious of the prosperity of the proud and wicked. So God's people are dismayed and confused, and drink it all in. 13 Have I been wasting my time? Why take the trouble to be pure? 14 All I get out of it is trouble and woe—every day and all day long.

(b)   17 Then one day I went into God's sanctuary to meditate, and thought about the future. . . . 18 Suddenly . . . 22 I saw myself so stupid and so ignorant; I must seem like an animal to you, O God. 23 But even so you love me! You are holding my right hand! 24 You will keep on guiding me all my life with your wisdom and counsel; and afterwards receive me into the glories of heaven! 25 Whom have I in heaven but you? And I desire no one on earth as much as you!

(c)   My health fails; my spirits droop, yet God remains! He is the strength of my heart; he is mine forever! 28 I will get as close to him as I can! I have chosen him and I will tell everyone about the wonderful ways he rescues me.

PSALM 74

12 God is my King from ages past; you have been actively helping me everywhere. 19 O Lord, save me!

PSALM 75

1 How we thank you, Lord! Your mighty miracles give proof that you care. 9 I shall forever declare the praises . . . of God. . . .

PSALM 76

(a)   1 God's reputation is very great. . . . 4 The everlasting mountains cannot compare with you in glory! 11 Fulfill all your vows that you have made to . . . your God.

PSALM 77

(a)   1 I cry to the Lord; I . . . call to him. . . . 2 I am in deep trouble and I need his help so badly. All night long I pray, lifting my hands to heaven, pleading. There can be no joy until he acts.

(b)   11 I recall the many miracles he did for me so long ago. 12 Those wonderful deeds are constantly in my thoughts. I cannot stop thinking about them. 13 O God, your ways are holy. Where is there any other as mighty as you? 14 You are the God of miracles and wonders! You still demonstrate your awesome power. 15 You have redeemed us.

PSALM 79

8 Let your tenderhearted mercies meet our needs. . . . 9 Help us, God of our salvation! Help us. . . . Oh, save us and forgive our sins. 11 Demonstrate the greatness of your power by saving them. 13 We your people . . . will thank you forever and forever, praising your greatness from generation to generation.

PSALM 80

1 O God . . . listen as I plead. Display your power and radiant glory. 2 Use your mighty power to rescue us. 3 O God. Look . . . on us in joy and love; only then shall we be saved. 14 Come . . . we beg of you, O God . . . and bless us. 17 Strengthen the man you . . . love, 18 we will never forsake you again. Revive us to trust in you. 19 Look . . . on us, your face aglow with joy and love.

PSALM 81

1 The Lord makes us strong! Sing praises! Sing to . . . God. 14 For God has given us these times of joy. . . . 5 I heard an unknown voice that said, 6 "Now I will relieve your shoulder of its burden; I will free your hands from their heavy tasks." 7 He said, "You cried to me in trouble and I saved you; I answered

. . . 8 Listen to me, O my people . . . O . . .
if you will only listen! 10 Only test me! Open your
mouth . . . and see if I won't fill it. You will receive
every blessing you can use! 13 Oh, that my people
would listen to me! Oh, that Israel would follow me,
walking in my paths."

PSALM 84

(a)   1 How lovely is your Temple, O Lord. . . . 2 I
long . . . to be able to enter your courtyard and come
near to the Living God. 4 How happy are those who
live in your Temple, singing your praises. 5 Happy are
those who are strong in the Lord, who want above all
else to follow your steps. 6 When they walk through
the Valley of Weeping it will become a place of springs
where pools of blessing and refreshment collect after
rains! 7 They will grow constantly in strength and each
of them is invited to meet with the Lord. . . . 8 O
. . . God . . . hear my prayer! Listen . . . 10 A
single day spent in your Temple is better than a thous-
and anywhere else! I would rather be a doorman of
the Temple . . . than live in palaces of wickedness.

(b)   11 For God is our Light and our Protector. He
gives us grace and glory. No good thing will he withhold from those who walks along his paths. 12 O
Lord . . . blessed are those who trust in you.

PSALM 85

(a)   1 Lord, you have poured out amazing blessings on
this land! 4 Now bring us back to loving you, O Lord.
. . . 6 Oh, revive us! Then your people can rejoice
in you again. 7 Pour out your love and kindness on
us, Lord, and grant us your salvation.

(b)   8 I am listening carefully to all the Lord is saying—
for he speaks to his people, his saints. . . . 9 Surely
his salvation is near to those who reverence him; our
land will be filled with his glory. 10 Mercy and truth
have met together. Grim justice and peace have kissed!
11 Truth rises from the earth and righteousness smiles
down from heaven. 12 Yes, the Lord pours down his
blessings on the land. . . . 13 Justice goes before him
to make a pathway for his steps.

PSALM 86

(a)   1 Hear my prayer, O Lord, and answer me, for I am
deep in trouble. 2 Protect me. . . . Save me . . .
I am . . . trusting you. 3 Be merciful, O Lord . . .
I am looking . . . to you in constant hope. 4 Give me
happiness, O Lord. . . . 5 O Lord, you are so good and
kind, so ready to forgive; so full of mercy for all who ask
your aid. 6 Listen . . . to my prayer, O God. Hear
my urgent cry. 7 I will call to you whenever trouble
strikes, and you will help me. 9 All . . . will . . .
bow before you, Lord, and praise your great and holy
name. 10 For you are great. . . . You alone are God.

(b)   11 Tell me where you want me to go and I will go
there. May every fiber of my being unite in reverence
to your name. 12 With all my heart I will praise you.
I will give glory to your name forever, 13 for you love
me so much! You are constantly so kind! You have rescued me from deepest hell. 15 You are merciful and
gentle, Lord . . . full of constant lovingkindness and
of truth; 16 so . . . grant strength to your servant and
save me.

PSALM 88

1 O . . . God of my salvation, I have wept before
you day and night. 2 Hear my prayers; oh, listen to my

cry, 3 for my life is full of troubles. . . . 9 My eyes
grow dim with weeping. Each day I beg your help; O
Lord, I reach my pleading hands to you for mercy.
13 O Lord, I plead for my life.

PSALM 89

(a)   1 Forever and ever I will sing about the tender kindness of the Lord! Young and old shall hear about your
blessings. 2 Your love and kindness are forever; your
truth is as enduring as the heavens. 3, 4 The Lord says,
"I have made a solemn agreement with my . . . servants. . . . I have taken an oath to establish his de-
scendants as kings forever on his throne, from now until eternity!" 6 Who . . . can be compared with God?
What . . . is anything like him? 7 Who is as revered
as he? 8 Faithfulness is your very character.

(b)   11 The heavens are yours, the world, everything—
for you created them all. 13 Strong is your arm!
Strong . . . lifted high in glorious strength.
14, 15 Your throne is founded on two strong pillars—
the one is Justice and the other Righteousness. Mercy
and Truth are your attendants. Blessed are those who
hear the joyful blast of your trumpet, for they shall
walk in the light of your presence. 16 They rejoice
all day long in your wonderful reputation and in your
perfect righteousness. 17 You are their strength. What
glory! . . . 18 Our protection is from the Lord himself. . . . 52 Blessed be the Lord forever! Amen!

PSALM 90 (KJV)

(a)   1 O Lord, thou hast been our dwelling place in all
generations. 2 Before the mountains were brought
forth, or ever thou hadst formed the earth and the
world, even from everlasting to everlasting thou art God.

(b)   3 Thou . . . sayest, Return, ye children of men.

4 For a thousand years in thy sight are but as yesterday when it is past. 5 They are as a sleep. . . . They are like grass which groweth up. In the morning it flourish-eth, and groweth up; in the evening it . . . withereth. 11 Who knoweth thy power? 12 So teach us to num-ber our days that we may apply our hearts unto wisdom.

(c)   13 Return, O Lord. How long? 14 O satisfy us early with thy mercy; that we may rejoice and be glad all our days. 16 Let thy work appear unto thy servants and thy glory unto their children. 17 Let the beauty of the Lord our God be upon us: and establish thou the works of our hands establish thou it.

PSALM 91 (KJV)

(a)   1 He that dwelleth in the secret place of the most High shall abide under the shadow of the Almighty. 2 I will say of the Lord, He is my refuge and my for-tress: my God; in him will I trust. 3 Surely he shall deliver thee. 4 He shall cover thee with his feathers, and under his wings shalt thou trust; his truth shall be thy shield. 5 Thou shalt not be afraid . . . 9 be-cause thou hast made the Lord . . . thy habitation. 11 He shall give his angels charge over thee, to keep thee in all thy ways. 12 They shall bear thee up.

(b)   (The Lord says) "Because he hath set his love upon me, therefore will I deliver him: I will be with him in trouble; I will deliver him and honour him. With long life will I satisfy him and show him my salvation.

PSALM 92

(a)   1 It is good to say, "Thank you" to the Lord, to sing praises to God. . . . 2 Every morning tell him, "Thank you for your kindness," and every evening re-joice in all his faithfulness. 3 Sing his praises. . . .

4 You have done so much for me, O Lord. No wonder I am glad! I sing for joy. 5 O Lord, what miracles you do! And how deep are your thoughts! 6 Unthinking people do not understand them! . . . 8 The Lord continues forever. . . . 10 You have made me strong. . . . How refreshed I am by your blessings!

(b)   12 The godly shall flourish . . . and grow. . . . 13 For they are transplanted into the Lord's own garden, and are under his personal care. Even in old age they will still produce fruit and be vital and green. 15 This honors the Lord, and exhibits his faithful care. He is my shelter. There is nothing but goodness in him.

PSALM 93

1, 2 Jehovah is King! He is robed in majesty and strength. The world is his throne. O Lord, you have reigned from prehistoric times, from the everlasting past. 3 The mighty oceans seem to thunder your praise. 5 Your royal decrees cannot be changed. Holiness is forever . . . keynote of your reign.

PSALM 94

(a)   1 Lord God . . . let your glory shine out. 10 He knows everything—doesn't he also know what you are doing? 11 The Lord is fully aware of how limited and futile the thoughts of mankind are, 12, 13 so he helps us. . . . This makes us follow his paths. . . .

(b)   14 The Lord will not forsake his people, for they are his prize. 15 Judgment will again be just and all the upright will rejoice. 16 Who will protect me? Who will be my shield? 17 I would have died unless the Lord had helped me. 18 I screamed, "I'm slipping, Lord!" and he was kind and saved me. 19 Lord, when doubts fill my mind, when my heart is in turmoil, quiet me and give me renewed hope and cheer. 21, 22 The Lord . . .

is my . . . mighty Rock where I can hide.

PSALM 95

1 Oh, come, let us sing to the Lord! Give a joyous shout in honor of the Rock of our salvation! 2 Come before him with thankful hearts. Let us sing him psalms of praise. 3 For the Lord is a great God. . . . 6 Come, kneel before the Lord our Maker, 7 for he is our God. . . . Oh, that we would hear him calling us today and come to him! 8 Don't harden your hearts.

PSALM 96

(a)   1 Sing a new song to the Lord! Sing it everywhere around the world! 2 Sing out his praises! Bless his name. Each day tell someone that he saves. 3 Publish his glorious acts throughout the earth. Tell everyone about the amazing things he does. 4 For the Lord is great beyond description, and greatly to be praised. Worship only him. . . . 5 Our God made the heavens! 6 Honor and majesty surround him; strength and beauty are in his Temple.

(b)   7 O nations of the world, confess that God alone is glorious and strong. 8 Give him the glory he deserves! . . . Come to worship him. 9 Worship the Lord with the beauty of holy lives. 10 Tell the nations that Jehovah reigns! He rules the world. His power can never be overthrown. He will judge all nations fairly. 11 Let the heavens be glad, the earth rejoice; let the vastness of the roaring seas demonstrate his glory. 12 Praise him for the growing fields, for they display his greatness. The trees in the forest rustle with praise.

PSALM 97

1 Jehovah is King! Let all the earth rejoice! Tell the farthest islands to be glad. 6 The heavens declare his

perfect righteousness; every nation sees his glory.
8, 9 All . . . have heard of your justice, Lord, and
are glad that you reign in majesty over the entire earth.
. . . 10 The Lord loves . . . the lives of his people,
and rescues them. . . . 11 Light is sown for the godly
and joy for the good. 12 May all who are godly be
happy in the Lord and crown him, our holy God.

PSALM 98

(a)   1 Sing a new song to the Lord telling about his
mighty deeds! For he has won a mighty victory by his
power and holiness. 2, 3 He has announced this victory and revealed it to every nation by fulfilling his
promise to be kind. . . . The whole earth has seen
God's salvation of his people. 4 That is why the earth
breaks out in praise to God, and sings for utter joy!

(b)   5 Sing your praise. . . . 6 Make a joyful symphony
before the Lord, the King! 7 Let the earth and all those
living on it shout, "Glory to the Lord." 8, 9 Let the
waves clap their hands . . . the hills sing out their
songs of joy before the Lord.

PSALM 99

1 Jehovah is King! . . . 3 Let them reverence
your great and holy name. 4 This mighty King is
determined to give justice. Fairness is the touchstone
of everything he does. He gives justice. . . . 5 Exalt
the Lord, our holy God! . . . 8 O . . . our God!
You answered them and forgave their sins. . . .
9 Exalt the Lord our God, and worship . . . for he is
holy.

PSALM 100 (KJV)

1 Make a joyful noise unto the Lord, all ye lands.
2 Serve the Lord with gladness: come before his pres-

ence with singing. 3 Know ye that the Lord he is God: it is he who hath made us and not we ourselves; we are his people. 4 Enter into his gates with thanksgiving, and into his courts with praise: be thankful unto him, and bless his name. 5 For the Lord is good; his mercy is everlasting; and his truth endureth to all generations.

PSALM 101

(a)   1 I will sing about your lovingkindness and your justice, Lord. I will sing your praises! 2 I will try to walk a blameless path, but how I need your help, especially in my own home, where I long to act as I should.

(b)   3 Help me to refuse the low and vulgar things; help me to abhor all crooked deals of every kind, to have no part in them. 4 I will reject all selfishness and stay away from every evil. 5 I will not listen to anyone who secretly slanders his neighbors; I will not permit conceit or pride. 6 I will make the godly . . . my heroes and invite them into my home.

PSALM 102

(a)   1 Lord, hear my prayer! Listen to my plea! 2 Give me speedy answers, 3 for my days disappear like smoke. . . . 7 I lie awake, lonely. . . . 9 My tears run down. . . . 11 My life is passing swiftly as the evening shadows. . . . 12 Lord . . . your famine will endure to every generation. 13 I know that you will come and have mercy . . . and now is the time. . . .

(b)   17 He will listen to the prayers of the destitute, for he is never too busy to heed their requests. 18 I am recording this so that future generations will also praise the Lord for all that he has done. A people that shall be created shall praise the Lord. 19 Tell them that God . . . 20 heard the groans of his people . . . and released them. 24 "O God, you live forever and forever!

26 You go on forever. . . . 27 You . . . never grow old. You are forever, and your years never end.

PSALM 103 (KJV)

(a)   1 Bless the Lord, O my soul, and all that is within me, bless his holy name. 2 Bless the Lord, O my soul, and forget not all his benefits: 3 who forgiveth all thine iniquities; who healeth . . . diseases; 4 who redeemeth thy life from destruction; who crowneth thee with lovingkindness and tender mercies; 5 who satisfieth thy mouth with good things; so that thy youth is renewed.

(b)   6 The Lord executeth righteousness and judgment for all that are oppressed. 8 The Lord is merciful and gracious, slow to anger, and plenteous in mercy. 10 He hath not dealt with us after our sins; nor rewarded us according to our iniquities. 11 For as the heaven is high above the earth, so great is his mercy toward them that reverence him. 12 As far as the east is from the west, so far hath he removed our transgressions from us. 13 Like a father pitieth his children, so the Lord pitieth them that [reverence] him. 14 For he knoweth our frame; he remembereth that we are dust.

(c)   As for man, his days are as grass: as a flower of the field, so he flourisheth. 16 The wind passeth over it and it is gone; and the place thereof shall know it no more.

(d)   17 But the mercy of the Lord is from everlasting to everlasting upon them that [reverence] him, and his righteousness unto children's children. 18 To such as keep his covenant, and to those who remember his commandments to do them. 19 The Lord hath prepared his throne in the heavens; and his kingdom ruleth over all.

(e)   20 Bless the Lord, ye . . . that do his commandments, hearkening unto the voice of his word. 21, 22 Bless ye the Lord, . . . all his works in all places of his dominion: bless the Lord, O my soul.

PSALM 104

(a)   1 I bless the Lord: O Lord my God, how great you are! Your are robed with honor and with majesty and light! 5 You bound the world together so that it would never fall apart. 24 O Lord, what a variety you have made! And in wisdom you have made them all! The earth is full of your riches.

(b)   31 Praise God forever! How he must rejoice in all his work! 33 I will sing to the Lord as long as I live. I will praise God to my last breath! 34 May he be pleased by all these thoughts about him, for he is the source of all my joy. 35 I will praise him. Hallelujah!

PSALM 105

1 Thank the Lord for all the glorious things he does; proclaim them to the nations. 2 Sing his praises and tell everyone about his miracles. 3 Glory in the Lord; O worshipers of God, rejoice. 4 Search for him and for his strength, and keep on searching! 5, 6 Think of the mighty deeds he did for us. . . . 7 He is the Lord our God. His goodness is seen everywhere. . . . 8, 9 Though a thousand generations pass he never forgets his promise.

PSALM 106

(a)   1 Hallelujah! Thank you, Lord! How good you are! Your love for us continues on forever. 2 Who can ever list the glorious miracles of God? Who can ever praise him half enough? 3 Happiness comes to those who are fair to others and are always just and good.

(b)   4 Remember me too, O Lord, while you are blessing and saving your people. 5 Let me too share in your chosen ones' prosperity and rejoice in all their joys, and receive the glory you give to them. 47 O Lord God, save us! . . .

(c)   48 Blessed be the Lord . . . God . . . from everlasting to everlasting. Let all the people say, "Amen!" Hallelujah!

PSALM 107

(a)   1 Say "Thank you" to the Lord for being so good, for . . . being so loving and kind. 2 Has the Lord redeemed you? Then speak out! Tell others he has saved you. . . . 3 He brought the exiles back. . . . 4 They were homeless . . . 6 "Lord, help!" they cried, and he did! 7 He led them straight to safety. . . . 8 Oh, that these men would praise the Lord for his lovingkindness, and for all his wonderful deeds! 9 For he satisfies the thirsty soul and fills the hungry soul with good.

10 Who are these who sit in darkness, in the shadow of death, crushed by misery and slavery? 13 They cried to the Lord in their troubles, and he rescued them! He led them from the darkness and shadow of death and snapped their chains. 15 Oh, that these men would praise the Lord for his lovingkindness and for all of his wonderful deeds!

(c)   17 Others . . . were ill. . . . 18 Their appetites were gone and death was near. 19 Then they cried to the Lord in their troubles, and he helped them and delivered them. 20 He spoke, and they were healed— snatched from the door of death. 21 Oh, that these men would praise the Lord for his lovingkindness and for all of his wonderful deeds! 22 Let them tell him "Thank you" . . . and sing about his glorious deeds.

(d)   23 And then there are the sailors. . . . 24 They, too, observe the power of God in action. 25 The waves rise high. 26 Their ships are tossed to the heavens and sink again to the depths; the sailors cringe in terror. 27 They reel and stagger . . . and are at their wit's end.

28 Then they cry to the Lord in their trouble, and he saves them. 29 He calms the storm and stills the waves. 30 What a blessing is that stillness, as he brings them safely into harbor!

(e)   31 Oh, that these men would praise the Lord for his lovingkindness and for all his wonderful deeds! 32 Let them praise him publicly before the congregation, and before the leaders of the nation. 38 How he blesses them! . . . 42 Good men everywhere will see it and be glad. . . . 43 Listen, if you are wise, to what I am saying. Think about the lovingkindness of the Lord!

PSALM 108

(a)   1 O God, my heart is ready to praise you! I will sing and rejoice before you. 2 Wake up. . . . We will meet the dawn with song. 3 I will praise you everywhere around the world, in every nation. 4 For your lovingkindness is great beyond measure, high as the heavens. Your faithfulness reaches the skies. 5 His glory is far more vast than the heavens. . . .

(b)   6 Hear the cry of your . . . child—come with mighty power and rescue me. 7 God has given sacred promises; no wonder I exult! 10 Who but God can give me strength? 13 With the help of God we shall do mighty acts of valour.

PSALM 109

(a)   21 O Lord, deal with me as your child, as one who bears your name! Because you are so kind, O Lord, deliver me. 26 Help me, O Lord my God! Save me. . . . 27 Do it publicly, so all will see that you yourself have done it.

(b)   30 I will give repeated thanks to the Lord, praising him to everyone. 31 He stands beside the poor and hungry to save them.

PSALM 110

1 Jehovah said to . . . the Messiah, "Rule as my
regent. . . . " 2 Jehovah has established your throne.
. . . 3 In that day . . . your people shall come to
you willingly, dressed in holy . . . robes. . . .
4 Jehovah has taken oath, and will not rescind his vow,
that you are a priest forever. . . . 6 God stands beside
you.

PSALM 111

(a) 1, 2 Hallelujah! I want to express publicy before
his people my heartfelt thanks to God for his mighty
miracles. All who are thankful should ponder them
with me. 3 For his miracles demonstrate his honor,
majesty, and eternal goodness. 4 Who can forget the
wonders he performs—deeds of mercy and of grace?
5 He gives food to those who trust him; he never forgets his promises. 6 He has shown his great power to
his people.

(b) 7 All he does is just and good, and all his laws are
right, 8 for they are formed from truth and goodness,
and stand firm forever. 9 He has paid full ransom for
his people; now they are always free to come to Jehovah (what a holy, awe-inspiring name that is).

(c) 10 How can men be wise? The only way to begin
is by reverence for God. For growth in wisdom comes
from obeying his laws. Praise his name forever.

PSALM 112

(a) 1 Praise the Lord! For all who fear God and trust
in him are blessed beyond expression. Yes, happy is
the person who delights in doing his commands.
2 His children shall be honored everywhere, for good
men's sons have a special heritage. 3 His good deeds
will never be forgotten. 4 When darkness overtakes

him, light will come bursting in. He is kind and merciful— 5 and all goes well for the generous man. . . .

(b)   6 God's constant care of him will make a deep impression on all who see it. 7 He does not fear bad
news, nor live in dread of what may happen. For he is
settled in his mind that Jehovah will take care of him.
8 That is why he is not afraid. . . .

(c)   9 He gives generously to those in need. His deeds
will never be forgotten. He shall have influence and
honor.

PSALM 113

1 Hallelujah! O servants of Jehovah, praise his name.
2 Blessed is his name forever and forever. 3 Praise him
from sunrise to sunset! 4 For he is high above the nations; his glory is far greater than the heavens. 5 Who
can be compared with God? 9 Hallelujah! Praise the
Lord.

PSALM 115

1 Glorify your name, not ours, O Lord! Cause everyone to praise your lovingkindness and your truth. 3 He
is in the heavens, and does as he wishes. 9 Trust the
Lord! He is your helper. He is your shield. 11 All of
you, his people, trust in him. He is your helper; he is
your shield. 12 Jehovah is constantly thinking about
us and he will surely bless us. He will bless . . .
13 all, both great and small, who reverence him.
14 May the Lord richly bless both you and your children. 15 Yes, Jehovah who made heaven and earth
will personally bless you! 17 The dead cannot sing
praises to Jehovah here on earth, 18 but we can! We
praise him forever! Hallelujah! Praise the Lord.

PSALM 116

(a)   1 I love the Lord because he hears my prayers and

79

answers them. 2 Because he . . . listens, I will pray as long as I breathe! 3 Death stared me in the face—I was frightened and sad. 4 Then I cried, "Lord, save me!" 5 How kind he is! How good he is! So merciful, this God of ours! 6 The Lord protects the simple and the childlike; I was facing death and then he saved me. 8 He has saved me from death, my eyes from tears, my feet from stumbling. 9 I shall live! Yes, in his presence—here on earth!

(b)   12 What can I offer Jehovah for all he has done for me? 13 I will bring him an offering . . . and praise his name for saving me. 15 His loved one are very precious to him. . . .

(c)   16 O Lord, you have freed me from my bonds and I will serve you forever. 17 I will worship you and offer you . . . thanksgiving. 18, 19 Here . . . before all the people, I will pay everything I vowed to the Lord. Praise the Lord.

PSALM 117

1 Praise the Lord, all nations everywhere. Praise him, all the peoples of the earth. 2 For he loves us very dearly, and his truth endures. Praise the Lord.

PSALM 118 (KJV)

(a)   1 O give thanks unto the Lord; for he is good: because his mercy endureth for ever. 4 Let them now who [revere] the Lord say, that his mercy endureth for ever.

(b)   5 I called upon the Lord in distress: the Lord answered me, and set me in a large place. 6 The Lord is on my side; I will not fear. What can man do unto me? 7 The Lord taketh my part with them that help me. 8 It is better to trust in the Lord than to put confidence in man.

(c) 14 The Lord is my strength and song, and is become my salvation. 15 The voice of rejoicing and salvation is in the [Church] of the righteous. 16 The right hand of the Lord doeth valiantly. 17 I shall . . . live and declare the works of the Lord. 18 The Lord hath . . . not given me over to death. 19 Open to me the gates of righteousness: I will go into them, and I will praise the Lord: 20 This gate of the Lord, into which the righteous shall enter. 21 I will praise thee: for thou hast heard me, and art become my salvation. The stone which the builders refused is become the head stone of the corner. 23 This is the Lord's doing; it is marvellous in our eyes. 24 This is the day which the Lord hath made; we will rejoice and be glad in it. Save now, I beseech thee, O Lord: O Lord, I beseech thee. 26 Blessed be he that cometh in the name of the Lord: 27 God is the Lord which hath shown us light: 28 Thou art my God, and I will exalt thee. 29 O give thanks unto the Lord; for he is good: for his mercy endureth for ever.

PSALM 119

(a) 1 Happy are all who perfectly follow the laws of God. 2 Happy are all who search for God, and always do his will, 3 rejecting compromise with evil, and walking only in his paths. 4 You have given us your laws to obey— 5 oh, how I want to follow them consistently. 6 Then I will not be disgraced, for I will have a clean record.

7 After you have corrected me I will thank you by living as I should! 8 I will obey! Oh, don't . . . let me slip back into sin again.

9 How can a young man stay pure? By reading your

Word and following its rules. 10 I have tried my best to find you—don't let me wander off from your instructions. 11 I have thought much about your words, and then stored them in my heart so that they would hold me back from sin.

12 Blessed Lord, teach me your rules. 13 I have recited your laws, 14 and rejoiced in them more than riches. 15 I will meditate upon them and give them my full respect. 16 I will delight in them and not forget them.

17 Bless me with life so that I can continue to obey you. 18 Open my eyes to see wonderful things in your Word. 19 I am but a pilgrim here on earth: how I need a map—and your commands are my chart and guide. 20 I long for your instructions more than I can tell.

23 I will continue in your plans. 24 Your laws are both my light and my counselors.

(b) 25 I am completely discouraged—I lie in the dust. Revive me by Your Word. 26 I told you my plans and you replied. Now give me your instructions. 27 Make me understand what you want; for then I shall see your miracles.

28 I weep with grief; my heart is heavy with sorrow; encourage and cheer me with your words. 29, 30 Keep me from every wrong; help me, undeserving as I am, to obey your laws, for I have chosen to do right. 31 I cling to your commands and follow them as closely as I can. Lord, don't let me make a mess of things. 32 If you will only help me to want your will, then I will follow your laws even more closely.

33, 34 Just tell me what to do and I will do it, Lord. As long as I live I'll wholeheartedly obey. 35 Make me walk along the right paths for I know how delightful they really are.

36 Help me to prefer obedience to making money!

37 Turn me away from wanting any other plan than yours. Revive my heart toward you. 38 Reassure me that your promises are for me, for I trust and revere you.

39 Your laws are right and good. 40, 41, 42 I long to obey them! Renew my life . . . yes, Lord, . . . I trust your promises.

43 May I never forget your words; for they are my only hope. 44, 45, 46 Therefore I will keep on obeying you forever and forever, free within the limits of your laws. I will speak . . . about their value, and they will listen with interest and respect.

47 How I love your laws! How I enjoy your commands! 48 "Come, come to me," I call to them, for I love them and will let them fill my life.

49, 50 Your promises to me, your servant . . . are my only hope. They give me strength in all my troubles; how they refresh and revive me! 51 Proud men hold me in contempt for obedience to God, but I stand unmoved. 52 I have tried to obey you; your Word has been my comfort.

54 These laws of yours have been my source of joy and singing through all these years of my earthly pilgrimage. 55 I obey them even at night and keep my thoughts, O Lord, on you. 56 What a blessing this has been to me—to constantly obey.

57 Jehovah is mine! And I promise to obey! With all my heart I want your blessings. Be merciful just as you promised. 59, 60 I thought about the wrong direction in which I was headed and turned around and came running back to you. 61 I am firmly anchored to your laws.

62 At midnight I will rise to give my thanks to you for your good laws. 63 Anyone is my brother who fears and trusts the Lord and obeys him. 64 O Lord,

the earth is full of your lovingkindness! Teach me your good paths.

65 Lord, I am overflowing with your blessings, just as you promised. 66 Now teach me good judgment as well as knowledge. For your laws are my guide. 67 I used to wander off; now I closely follow all you say. 68 You are good and do only good; make me follow your lead.

69 I obey your laws with all my heart.

71, 72 The punishment you gave me was the best thing that could have happened to me, for it taught me to pay attention to your laws. They are more valuable to me than millions in silver and gold!

73 You made my body, Lord; now give me sense to heed your laws. 74 All those who fear and trust in you will welcome me because I too am trusting in your Word.

75, 76, 77 I know, O Lord, that your decisions are right and that your punishment was right and did me good. Now let your lovingkindness comfort me, just as you promised. Surround me with your tender mercies, that I may live. Your law is my delight.

78 I will concentrate my thoughts upon your laws.

79 Let all others join me, who trust and fear you, and we will discuss your laws. 80 Help me to love your every wish; then I will never have to be ashamed of myself.

81 I grow faint for your salvation; but I expect your help, for you have promised it. 82 My eyes are straining to see your promises come true. . . . 83 I cling to your laws and obey them. 86 Help me, for you love only truth.

89 Forever, O Lord, your Word stands firm in heaven. 90, 91 Your faithfulness extends to every generation, like the earth you created; it endures by your de-

cree, for everything serves your plans.

92 I would have despaired and perished unless your laws had been my deepest delight. 93 I will never lay aside your laws, for you have used me to restore my joy and health. 94 I am yours! Save me! For I have tried to live according to your desires. 95 I will quietly keep my mind on your promises.

96 Nothing is perfect except your words. 97 Oh, how I love them. I think about them all day long. 98 They make me wiser . . . because they are my constant guide. 99 Yes, wiser than my teachers, for I am ever thinking of your rules. 100 They make me even wiser than the aged.

101 I have refused to walk the paths of evil for I will remain obedient to your Word. 102, 103 No, I haven't turned away from what you taught me; your words are sweeter than honey. 104 Only your rules can give me wisdom and understanding. . . . 105 Your words are a flashlight to light the path ahead of me, and keep me from stumbling. 106 I've said it once and I'll say it again: I will obey these wonderful laws of yours.

108 Accept my grateful thanks and teach me your desires. 109 I will not give up obedience to your laws. 111 Your laws are my joyous treasure forever. 112 I am determined to obey you until I die.

113 I hate those who are undecided whether or not to obey you; but my choice is clear—I love your law. 114 You are my refuge and my shield, and your promises are my only source of hope.

118 All who reject your laws . . . are only fooling themselves.

123 My eyes grow dim with longing for you to fulfill your wonderful promise. 124 Lord, deal with me in lovingkindness, and teach me, your servant, to obey;

125 for I am your servant; therefore give me common sense to apply your rules to everything I do.

128 Every law of God is right, whatever it concerns. . . .

129 Your laws are wonderful; no wonder I obey them. 130 As your plan unfolds, even the simple can understand it. 131 No wonder I wait expectantly for each of your commands.

132 Come and have mercy on me as is your way with those who love you. 133 Guide me with your laws so that I will not be overcome by evil. 135 Look . . . in love upon me and teach me all your laws.

137 O Lord, you are just and . . . fair. 138 Your demands are just and right. 140 I have thoroughly tested your promises and that is why I love them so much.

142 Your justice is eternal for your laws are perfectly fair. 143 In my distress and anguish, you commandments comfort me. 144 Your laws are always fair; help me to understand them and I shall live.

145 I am praying with great earnestness; answer me, O Lord, and I will obey your laws. 147 Early in the morning, before the sun is up, I am praying and reviewing how much I trust in you. 148 I stay awake through the night to think about your promises. 149 Because you are so loving and kind, listen to me and make me well again.

151 You are near, O Lord; all your commandments are based on truth. 152 I have known from earliest days that your will never changes. 156 Lord, how great is your mercy. . . .

159 Lord, see how much I really love you. . . . 160 There is utter truth in all your laws; your decrees are eternal.

161 I stand in awe of only your words. 162 I rejoice in your laws like one who finds a great treasure. 163 I

love your laws. 164 I will praise you because of your wonderful laws.

165 Those who love your laws have great peace of heart and mind and do not stumble. 166 I long for your salvation, Lord. . . . 167 I have looked for your commandments and I love them very much; 168 yes, I have searched for them. You know this because everything I do is known to you.

169 O Lord, listen to my prayers; give me common sense. . . . 170 Hear my prayers. . . . 171 I praise you for letting me learn your laws. 172 I will sing about their wonder, for each of them is just. 173 I have chosen to follow your will. 174 O Lord, I have longed for your salvation, and your law is my delight. 175 I will praise you; let your laws assist me.

176 I have wandered away like a lost sheep; come and find me.

PSALM 120

(a) 1 In my troubles I pled with God to help me and he did!

(b) 2 Deliver me, O Lord. . . . 7 I am for peace.

PSALM 121 (KJV)

1 I will lift up mine eyes unto the hills, from whence cometh my help. 2 My help cometh from the Lord who made heaven and earth. 3, 4 He will not suffer thy foot to be moved: he that keepeth thee will not slumber . . . nor sleep. 5 The Lord is thy keeper: the Lord is thy shade upon thy right hand. 6 The sun shall not smite thee by day, nor the moon by night. 7 The Lord shall preserve thee from all evil: he shall preserve thy soul. 8 The Lord shall preserve thy going out and thy coming in from this time forth, and even for evermore.

PSALM 122

(a)   1 I was glad for the suggestion of going . . . to the
      Temple. 4 Jehovah's people—have come to worship . .
      to thank and praise the Lord.

(b)   6 Pray for . . . peace. . . . 7 May there be peace
      . . . and prosperity. . . . 8 This I ask for . . . all
      my brothers. 9 May there be peace.

PSALM 123

      1 O God enthroned in heaven, I lift my eyes to you.
      2 We look to . . . our God for his mercy and kindness.
      . . . 3 Have mercy on us, Lord, have mercy.

PSALM 124

      1 If the Lord had not been on our side (let all . . .
      admit it), if the Lord had not been on our side,
      2, 3 we would have been swallowed alive by our
      enemies, destroyed by their anger. 4, 5 We would
      have drowned beneath the floor of these men's fury
      and pride. 6 Blessed be Jehovah who has not let
      them devour us. 8 Our help is from the Lord who
      made heaven and earth.

PSALM 125

      1 Those who trust in the Lord are steady . . . un-
      moved by any circumstance. 2 Just as the mountains
      surround and protect . . . so the Lord surrounds and
      protects his people. 4 Lord, do good to those who are
      good, whose hearts are right with the Lord. . . .

PSALM 126

(a)   1 It was like a dream! 2 How we laughed and sang
      for joy. . . "What amazing things the Lord has done
      for them." 3 Yes, glorious things! What wonder! What

joy!

(b)   5 Those who sow tears shall reap joy. 6 Yes, they go
out weeping, carrying seed for sowing, and return singing, carrying their sheaves [harvest].

PSALM 127

(a)   1 Unless the Lord builds a house, the builers' work
is useless. Unless the Lord protects a city, sentries do
no good. 2 It is senseless for you to work so hard from
early morning until late at night, fearing you will starve
to death; for God wants his loved ones to get their
proper rest.

(b)   3 Children are a gift from God; they are his reward.
5 Happy is the parent who has his quiver full of them.

PSALM 128

1 Blessings to all who reverence and trust the Lord—
on all who obey him! 2 Their reward shall be prosperity and happiness. 3 Your wife shall be contented
in your home. And look at all those children! There
they sit around the dinner table . . . vigorous and
healthy. . . . 4 That is God's reward to those who
reverence and trust him. 5 May the Lord continually
bless you with heaven's blessings as well as with human
joys. 6 May you live to enjoy your grandchildren!

PSALM 129

3, 4 The Lord is good. For he has snapped the
chains that . . . had bound me. . . . 8 "Jehovah's
blessings be upon you; we bless you in Jehovah's name."

PSALM 130

1 O Lord, from the depths of despair I cry for your help: 2 "Hear me! Answer! Help me!" 3, 4 Lord, if you kept in mind our sins then who could ever get an answer to his prayer? But you forgive! What an awesome thing this is! 5 That is why I wait expectantly, trusting God to help, for he has promised. 6 I long for him. . . . 7 . . . hope in the Lord; for he is loving and kind, and comes to us with armloads of salvation.

PSALM 131

1 Lord, I am not proud and haughty. I don't think myself better than others. I don't pretend to "know it all." 2 I am quiet now before the Lord. . . . 3 Quietly trust in the Lord—now, and always.

PSALM 132

(a) 1 Lord, do you remember that time when my heart was so filled with turmoil? 2 I couldn't rest, I couldn't sleep. . . . 5 Then I vowed that I would do it; I made a solemn promise to the Lord.

(b) 11 You will never go back on your promise! 14 You said, "I have always wanted it this way. 15 I will make this city prosperous and satisfy her poor with food."

PSALM 133

1 How wonderful it is, how pleasant, when brothers [and sisters] live in harmony! 2 Harmony is . . . precious. . . . 3 Harmony is . . . refreshing. . . . God has pronounced this eternal blessing . . . even life forevermore.

PSALM 134

1 Oh, bless the Lord, you who serve him. . . .

2 Lift your hands in holiness and bless the Lord.
3 The Lord bless you . . . the Lord who made
heaven and earth.

PSALM 135

1, 2 Hallelujah! Yes, let his people praise him. . . .
3 Praise the Lord because he is so good; sing to his
wonderful name. 5 I know the greatness of the Lord.
13 O Jehovah, your name endures forever; your fame
is known to every generation. 19 O . . . , bless
Jehovah! 20 Oh, bless his name, all of you who trust
and reverence him. 21 All . . . praise the Lord, for
he lives. Hallelujah!

PSALM 136

1 Oh, give thanks to the Lord, for he is good; his
lovingkindness continues forever. 4 Praise him who
alone does mighty miracles, . . . 16 who led his
people . . . 17 who saved his people. . . . 21 God
gave the land . . . as a gift forever, for his lovingkindness continues forever.

PSALM 137

5, 6 If I forget you, . . . let my right hand forget
its skill. . . . If I fail to love . . . more than my
highest joy, let me never sing again. 7 O Jehovah, do
not forget.

PSALM 138

(a)   1 Lord, with all my heart I thank you. I will sing
your praises. . . . 2 . . . I worship, giving thanks
to you for all your lovingkindness and your faithfulness, for your promises are backed by all the honor
of your name. 3 When I pray, you answer me, and
encourage me by giving me the strength I need.

(b)   5 Sing about Jehovah's glorious ways, for his glory is very great. 6 Yet though he is so great, he respects the humble. . . . 7 Though I am surrounded by troubles, you will bring me safely through them. . . . Your power will save me. The Lord will work out his plans for my life—for your lovingkindness, Lord, continues forever. . . . You made me.

PSALM 139 (KJV)

(a) 1 O Lord, thou hast searched me, and known me. 2 Thou knowest my downsitting and mine uprising, thou understandest my thoughts afar off. 3 Thou compassest my path and my lying down, and art acquainted with all my ways. 4 For there is not a word in my tongue, but, lo, O Lord, thou knowest it altogether. 5 Thou hast beset me behind and before, and laid thine hand upon me. 6 Such knowledge is too wonderful for me; it is high, I cannot attain unto it. 7 Whither shall I go from thy spirit? or whither shall I flee from thy presence? If I ascend up into heaven, thou art there. 9 If I take the wings of the morning, and dwell in the uttermost parts of the sea; 10 even there shall thy hand lead me, and thy right hand shall hold me. 11 If I say, Surely the darkness shall cover me; even the night shall be light about me. 12 Yea, the darkness hideth not from thee; but the night shineth as the day: the darkness and the light are both alike to thee.

(b) 13 Thou hast possessed my reins: thou hast covered me in my mother's womb. 14 I will praise thee; for I am fearfully and wonderfully made: marvellous are thy works; and that my soul knoweth right well. 15 My substance was not hid from thee, when I was made in secret, and curiously wrought. 16 Thine eyes did see my substance, yet being imperfect; and in thy book all my members were written, which in continuance were fashioned, when as yet there was none of them.

(c)   17 How precious also are thy thoughts unto me, O God! how great is the sum of them! 18 If I should count them, they are more in number than the sand: when I awake, I am still with thee. 23 Search me, O God, and know my heart: try me, and know my thoughts: 24 see if there be any wicked way in me, and lead me in the way everlasting.

PSALM 140

(a)   1 O Lord, deliver me. . . . Preserve me. . . . 6, 7 O . . . my Lord and Savior, my God and my shield—hear me as I pray!

(b)   12 The Lord will surely help. . . . He will maintain the rights of the poor. 13 Surely the godly are thanking you, for they shall live in your presence.

PSALM 141

1 Quick, Lord, answer me—for I have prayed. Listen when I cry to you for help! 2 Regard my prayer. . . . 3 Help me, Lord, to keep my mouth shut and my lips sealed. 4 Take away my lust for evil things; don't let me want to be with sinners, doing what they do, sharing their dainties. 5 Let the godly smite me! It will be kindness! If they reprove me, it is medicine! Don't let me refuse it. . . . 8 I look to you for help, O Lord God. You are my refuge. . . .

PSALM 142

(a)   1, 2 How I plead with God, how I implore his mercy, pouring out my troubles before him. 3 For I am overwhelmed and desperate, and you alone know which way I ought to turn. . . . 5 Then I prayed to Jehovah: "Lord, " I pled, "you are my only place of refuge.

Only you can keep me safe.

(b)   6 "Hear my cry, for I am very low. Rescue me from
my persecutors, for they are too strong for me. 7 The
godly will rejoice with me for all your help."

PSALM 143

(a)   1 Hear my prayer, O Lord; answer my plea, because
you are faithful to your promises. 2 As compared with
you, no one is perfect. 4 I am losing all hope; I am
paralyzed with fear. 6 I reach out for you. I thirst for
you. . . . 7 Come quickly, Lord, and answer me, for
my depression deepens. . . . 8 Let me see your kindness to me . . . for I am trusting you. Show me where
to walk, for my prayer is sincere.

(b)   9 O Lord, I run to you to hide me. 10 Help me to
do your will, for you are my God. Lead me in good
paths, for your Spirit is good. 11 Lord . . . bring me
out of all this trouble because you are true to your
promises. 12 You are loving and kind to me. . . .
I am your servant.

PSALM 144

(a)   1 Bless the Lord who is my immovable Rock. He
gives me skill in battle. 2 He is always kind and loving
to me. . . . He stands before me as a shield.

(b)   3 O Lord, what is mankind that you even notice him?
. . . 4 For man is but a breath; his days are like a passing shadow. 5 Lord, come. . . . 7 Rescue me; deliver me from deep waters. 9 I will sing you a new
song, O God. . . . 10 For you grant victory. . . .
You are the one who will rescue. . . . 11 Save me!
. . . 15 Happy are those whose God is the Jehovah.

PSALM 145

(a) 1, 2 I will praise you, my God and King, and bless your name each day and forever. 3 Great is Jehovah! Greatly praise him! His greatness is beyond discovery! 4 Let each generation tell its children what glorious things he does. 5 I will meditate about your glory, splendor, majesty, and miracles. 6 Your awe-inspiring deeds shall be on every tongue; I will proclaim your greatness. 7 Everyone will tell about how good you are, and sing about your righteousness.

(b) 8 Jehovah is kind and merciful, slow to get angry, full of love. 9 He is good to everyone, and his compassion is intertwined with everything he does. 10 All living things shall thank you, Lord, and your people will bless you. 11 They will talk together about the glory of your kingdom and mention examples of your power. 12 They will tell about your miracles and about the majesty and glory of your reign. 13 For your kingdom never ends. You rule generation after generation.

(c) 14 The Lord lifts the fallen and those bent beneath their loads. 15 The eyes of all mankind look up to you for help; you give them their food as they need it. 16 You constantly satisfy the hunger and thirst of every living thing. 17 The Lord is fair in everything he does, and full of kindness. 18 He is close to all who call on him sincerely. 19 He fulfills the desires of those who reverence and trust him; he hears their cries for help and rescues them.

(d) 20 He protects all those who love him. . . . 21 I will praise the Lord and call on all men everywhere to bless his holy name forever and forever.

PSALM 146

(a) 1 Praise the Lord! Yes, really praise him! 2 I will praise him as long as I live, yes, even with my dying breath. 3 Don't look to men for help; their greatest leaders fail; 4 for every man must die. His breathing stops, life ends, and in a moment all he planned for himself is ended. 5 But happy is the man who has . . . God . . . as his helper, whose hope is in the Lord his God— 6 the God who made both earth and heaven, the seas and everything in them.

(b)   He is the God who keeps every promise, 7 and gives justice to the poor and oppressed, and food to the hungry. He frees the prisoners, 8 and opens the eyes of the blind; he lifts the burdens from those bent down beneath their loads. For the Lord loves good men. 9 He protects the immigrants, and cares for orphans and widows. . . . 10 The Lord will reign forever. God is king in every generation. Hallelujah! Praise the Lord!

Psalm 147
(a)   1 Hallelujah! Yes, praise the Lord! How good it is to sing his praises! How delightful and how right! 3 He heals the brokenhearted, binding up their wounds He counts the stars and calls them all by name. 5 How great he is! His power is absolute! His understanding is unlimited. 6 The Lord supports the humble. . . . 7 Sing out your thanks to him; sing praises to our God. . . .

(b)   11 His joy is in those who reverence him, those who expect him to be loving and kind. 12 Praise him. . . . Praise God! 13 He has fortified your gates against all enemies. . . . 14 He sends peace. . . . 20 Hallelujah! Yes, praise the Lord!

PSALM 148

1 Praise the Lord. . . . Let everything he has made give praise to him. For he issued his command, and they came into being; 6 he established their existence forever and forever. . . . 13 All praise the Lord together. For he alone is worthy. His glory is far greater than all. . . . 14 Hallelujah! Yes, praise the Lord!

PSALM 149

1 Hallelujah! Yes, praise the Lord! Sing him a new song. Sing his praises, all his people. 2 Rejoice in your Maker. . . . 4, 5 For Jehovah enjoys his people; he will save the humble. Let his people rejoice in this honor. Let them sing for joy. . . . 6, 7 Adore him, O his people. 9 He is the glory of his people. Hallelujah! Praise him!

PSALM 150

1 Hallelujah! Yes, Praise the Lord! Praise him in his Temple, and in the heavens he made with mighty power. 2 Praise him for his mighty works. Praise his unequaled greatness. 6 Let everything alive give praises to the Lord! You praise him! Hallelujah!

PART THREE

How to Use
Silver in the Psalms

I. Nondirected Reading

I have indicated in Part One the genesis of *Silver in the Psalms*. The work originated in a personal need of mine for Bible devotional reading. I wanted an arrangement of the Psalms where I could read, from the beginning or from any point at which I chose to begin, only passages which were positive; or if negative, passages which would be capable of being resolved into a positive outcome.

I went into some detail concerning the reasons for these kinds of needs in my devotional reading in the Psalms. I stated that there might be many others who also had the same needs along these lines that I did—persons who might also be edified by the existence of a version such as this one. With the creation of *Silver in the Psalms,* I feel I have produced a way to read the Psalms in a nondirected way. By this, I mean that one can now begin reading at any point in the Psalms, with no goal or purpose in mind other than to receive a blessing and can proceed without fear of diversion, and with a heightened confidence that the end will be achieved. This, I feel, is a major way to use the work.

II. Theme Reading

There might be other occasions when a person would like to read in the Psalms about some specific theme. Now, this can also be accomplished by referring to the *Appendix* where I have attempted to group together passages under several different topics dealing with similar themes. This approach, then, would be a second major use of *Silver in the Psalms.*

The passages are referred to by psalm number and a letter designating the part of the psalm passage referred. Sometimes the reference presented there might be to a whole psalm, but other times it might refer only to a part of the psalm. I have subdivided many of the psalms into sections dealing with a somewhat similar theme. The effect has been to increase again the homogeneity of content of the psalm passages which have been selected for inclusion in *Silver in the Psalms,* thus making it a little easier to locate and to collect similar theme passages.

Of course, even the subdivision did not make each section totally homogeneous. There are so many intertwined and overlapped feelings and concepts in the Psalms that it is impossible to completely disentangle the themes. Such an attempt would have resulted in over-meticulous subdivisions. I have chosen rather to let the intermixed themes remain enmeshed and to let them be included alongside any reference to a particular theme. Because of this, the same passage may be cited under several different themes. But this will prove to be of little or no difficulty if one reads the passage with the mental set pointed toward the theme being read.

To illustrate how one theme can be disentangled mentally from the other themes which lie alongside that theme, I have taken the first reference in the *Appendix* and have presented each of the passages referred to there, with a commentary between each selection. The commentary is meant to focus on how we can tune ourselves into a particular theme and follow that one theme, without being turned aside from our purpose by other themes which arise within the selection. I have reacted to the theme personally, as the psychologist and Christian I am. That makes the passage more meaningful to me. I emphasize again the importance of making a *personal reaction* to the Psalms—indeed to all Scripture—in order to bring it home to where we live.

Psalm 30

6, 7 In my prosperity I said, "This is forever, nothing can stop me now! The Lord has shown me his favor. He has made me steady as a mountain." . . . Suddenly my courage was gone; I was terrified and panic-stricken. 8 I cried to you, O Lord; oh, how I pled: . . . 10 "Hear me, Lord; oh have pity and help me." 11 Then he turned my sorrow into joy! . . . 12 O Lord my God, I will keep on thanking you forever!

In this passage we hear the clear and distinct feelings of a total abandonment to one's fears. Panic leads to an anxiety attack, and the psalmist feels totally helpless. He turned to God as his resource and was steadied.

Psalm 40

1 I waited patiently for God to help me; then he heard my cry. He lifted me out of the pit of despair, out from the bog and the mire, and set my feet on a hard, firm path and steadied me as I walked along.

The key words and phrases to focus upon in this passage are "cry," "pit of despair," "bog," and "mire." When we are experiencing the panic of anxiety, we *do* feel bogged down and unable to move—frozen in indecision or vacillation. The feeling truly is existential despair. But God delivered this writer.

There is another passage in Psalm 40 which also echoes anxiety.

11 O Lord, don't hold back your tender mercies from me! My only hope is in your love and faithfulness. 12 Otherwise I perish, for problems far too big for me to solve are piled higher than my head. Meanwhile my sins, too many to count, have all caught up with me and I am ashamed to look up. My heart quails within me. 13 Please, Lord, rescue me! Quick! Come and help me!

It is not uncommon for persons suffering from anxiety also to experience many bodily symptoms such as heart palpitations or pains in the chest. The psalmist's heart "quailed" within him. He was able to identify the causes—too many unsolved problems to deal with, and personal anguish over past sins catching up with him. He actually stated that he had the feeling of being "caught up" with, and consequently he felt deeply ashamed. The problems awaiting resolution may or may not have been a part of his "sins"—we are not told; but together they were a formidable foe. He knew the truth—only God could help him then.

Psalm 55
1 Listen to my prayer, O God. . . . 2 Hear me, Lord! Listen to me! 6 Oh, for wings like a dove, to fly away and rest! 7 I would fly to far off deserts and stay there. 8 I would flee to some refuge from all this storm.

The psalmist's redundancy in pleading with God to hear him reflects the anguish of soul he was experiencing. At times like these, the anxious soul is not ready to problem-solve. There is only one thought—escape. Here is a graphic portrayal of the defensive device of detached fantasy. How rich would be the content if we were able to explore what was in the mind of the psalmist when he spoke of "some refuge."

Psalm 56

1 Lord, have mercy on me. . . . 3, 4 When I am afraid, I will put my confidence in you. Yes, I will trust the promises of God. And since I am trusting in him, what can mere man do to me? 8 You have collected all my tears and preserved them in your bottle! You have recorded every one in your book. 9 The very day I call for help, the tide . . . turns. . . . This one thing I know: God is for me! 10, 11 I am trusting God—oh, praise his promises! I am not afraid of anything mere man can do to me! Yes, praise his promises. 12 I will surely do what I have promised, Lord, and thank you for your help. 13 For you have saved me from death and my feet from slipping, so that I can walk before the Lord in the land of the living.

While the predominant mood of this passage is positive, slightly beneath the surface are echoes of anxiety—"when I am afraid"; "I am not afraid"; "saved me from death and my feet from slipping." God was surely an effective shield for this psalmist.

Psalm 61

1 O God, listen to me! Hear my prayer! 2 For wherever I am, though far away at the ends of the earth, I will cry to you for help. When my heart is faint and overwhelmed, lead me to the mighty, towering Rock of safety.

The psalmist here sounds a little "edgy." There is some panickiness and dis-ease about his statements of faith. He is certainly using God to defend himself from his fears. God is up to the task!

Psalm 62

   1 I stand silently before the Lord, waiting for him to rescue me. For salvation comes from him alone.
   2 Yes, he alone is my Rock, my rescuer, defense. . . . Why then should I be tense with fear when troubles come? 7 My protection and success come from God alone. He is my refuge, a Rock where no enemy can reach me.

This psalmist is encouraging himself with his faith as he rides out an anxiety storm. He tells his body to relax and tries to attain some perspective on his problems. He seems to say that success must be evaluated with reference to God-reality, and that troubles are reduced in their power when seen in the framework of God's dominion over things.

Psalm 91

   1 We live within the shadow of the Almighty, sheltered by the God who is above all. . . . 2 This I declare, that he alone is my refuge, he is my God, and I am trusting him. 4 He will shield you with his wings! They will shelter you. His faithful promises are your armor. 5 Now you don't need to be afraid of the dark any more, nor fear the dangers of the day. . . . Jehovah is my refuge! I choose . . . God . . . to shelter me. 10 How then can evil overtake me?

It is hard to see whether the psalmist is talking to others or to himself as he says, "Now you don't need to be afraid of the dark any more, nor fear the dangers of the day." His statement, however, is confident, indicating victory over such fears, real or neurotic.

Psalm 107

23 And then there are the sailors. . . . 24 They, too, observe the power of God in action. 25 The waves rise high. Their ships are tossed to the heavens and sink again to the depths; the sailors cringe in terror. 27 They reel and stagger . . . and are at their wit's end. 28 Then they cry to the Lord in their trouble, and he saves them. 29 He calms the storm and stills the waves. 30 What a blessing is that stillness, as he brings them safely into harbor!

Among a series of verbal mosaics which the psalmist presents in Psalm 107 is this symbolic picture of those who suffer anxiety. The significant statement to me is the contrast portrayed in the words, "What a blessing is that stillness." Relief is so beautiful. God can do that.

Psalm 112

6 God's constant care of him will make a deep impression on all who see it. 7 He does not fear bad news, nor live in dread of what may happen. For he is settled in his mind that Jehovah will take care of him. 8. That is why he is not afraid.

Here the psalmist speaks of the anti-anxiety effects of the awareness of God's care for his own. The effect is that "he is settled in his mind."

Psalm 119

25 I am completely discouraged—I lie in the dust. Revive me by your Word. 28 I weep with grief; my heart is heavy with sorrow; encourage and cheer me with your words. 72, 73 The punishment you gave me was the best thing that could have happened to me, for it taught me to pay attention to your laws.

Here are several verses, selected from this longest of all chapters in the Bible, which speak of anxiety and depression. The psalmist concludes in this selection of verses with the healing perspective of God's ways. He implies that when he focused attention upon God's laws, his other problems seemed less a disaster and more a stimulus to reorganization.

Psalm 132

1 Lord, do you remember that time when my heart was so filled with turmoil? I couldn't rest, I couldn't sleep. . . . 5 Then I vowed that I would do it; I made a solemn promise to the Lord.

Restlessness and sleep problems—so characteristic of the anxiety neurotic! The psalmist found that a least part of his "turmoil" was due to a free-floating, a lack of commitment. We can almost see resolution, reorientation, and re-motivation in his vow or promise.

Psalm 143

4 I am losing all hope; I am paralyzed with fear. 6 I reach out for you; I thirst for you. . . . 7 Come quickly, Lord, and answer me, for my depression deepens. . . . 8 Let me see your kindness to me . . . for I am trusting you. Show me where to walk, for my prayer is sincere. 9 O Lord, I run to you to hide me. 10 Help me to do your will, for you are my God. Lead me in good paths, for your Spirit is good. 11 Lord . . . bring me out of all this trouble because you are true to your promises. 12 You are loving and kind to me. . . . I am your servant.

I conclude this collection of passages, containing the themes of anxiety and depression, with a selection which is dominated by gloom. The psalmist, as he writes, is "paralyzed with fear," "losing hope," deepening in depression, and running to hide. But he is also reaching out, trusting and thirsting for God. He is kindling fires of warmth and healing, for his faith is strong and in the right direction. I would say the prognosis is good.

III. Labeling

Another very personal way to enjoy the Psalms is to read each psalm and try to give it a title. I have found in my devotional reading that, as I have read a psalm, sometimes a theme stood out so clearly that it seemed to be the obviously central theme of that psalm—*for me*. I want to emphasize once more the personal element, for what might be a very clear message to me might say nothing at all to someone else. It is *my* theme, coming out of *my* life experience, to meet *my* needs. My title might or might not correspond to the one you would perhaps select, but they could both be "correct" in that they are correct for each of us as individuals.

Of course, I am not speaking here of theological interpretation, but rather of the feelings produced in us as we read the Scripture passages in the Psalms. It could even be possible that we might agree on the theological interpretation of a passage, but because we were in two different places in our lives emotionally, we might identify two entirely different feelings in ourselves in response to the same passage, thus, coming up with very different titles. So, do not worry about whether your feeling-title is correct or incorrect; your feeling simply is! Don't try to be correct. Try to be real.

You might find that you experience about the same feeling when you reread a passage in the Psalms from time to time. This usually is because of your past history of the conditioning of your feeling to that psalm, but that's OK. This would merely mean that you had for that psalm a fairly stable feeling-association.

On the other hand, it might be that the feelings you had on one occasion, which led you to title the psalm as you chose to do then, on another occasion could be quite different because your perceptual standpoint had changed. You might then have a very different perspective as you read the passage, and because of this, your feeling-response would be quite different. But that is OK, too. You might need to change the old title you had previously assigned to it to one that would more accurately reflect your present feeling.

Some psalms contain enough verses around a central feeling-theme that they are homogeneous enough to permit a single title to represent the whole psalm. Many of the psalms, however, have several different themes within the same psalm, thus, making it difficult to focus on a theme. This could be handled in one of two different ways. First, you could subdivide the psalm, much as I have attempted to do in Part Two, and as is reflected in the *Appendix*. You could then give separate titles to each section. Or you could use as the temporary title for the whole psalm the one feeling-response which dominates your feeling, after having read the whole psalm.

Don't be afraid to listen to your feeling. Don't fear responding to your feelings, particularly when there is no fear of irresponsible acting out. We all can learn much from our feelings, but not until they are out in the open, experienced, and objectified for a later, more careful scrutiny and analysis by reason.

I want to share with you, as a model for your own exploration, some titles I have come up with as a result of my own feeling-responses to some of the psalms I have read. These, then, are the feelings I experienced, which I tried to encapsulate in a title, as I read the following psalms.

Psalm 1: The Beautiful Christian

Psalm 2: Tears He Hears

111

Psalm 121: Preservation

Psalm 126: Euphoric Victory!

Psalm 128: The Family Psalm

Psalm 133: Christian Fellowship

Psalm 139: The Omniscient Father

IV. Special Occasion Readings

There are yet many other ways *Silver in the Psalms* may be used. There are many occasions when a minister is called upon to select a passage of Scripture for use in a special service. Many times he chooses the Psalms. I know from personal experience that I have found myself caught in a slight dilemma at time. The problem has been this: should I read the whole passage, some of which is clearly not applicable, or should I risk doing so much skipping of verses that fellow readers either would not be able to follow the selection easily, or the reading would sound choppy to them if the verses were verbally identified. Usually I have wound up reading the whole passage, but have been disappointed with the impact I felt it made in the light of its possibilities.

More specifically, one psalm which is read quite often at funerals is Psalm 90. This song of Moses is a beautiful statement about the God of eternity, but when the whole passage is read, I (at least) am left with the feeling of the remoteness or sternness of God, something I do not experience as a Christian nor wish to communicate in the reading. I have found that by selecting verses for a consecutive reading in *Silver in the Psalms* I am able to circumvent this problem, and to have available for certain occasions this special rendition of the psalm.

Let me be even more specific in my illustration of how this work can be used in a variety of settings which call for the reading of a Scripture passage. I now present both the passages which have been selected for inclusion in *Silver in the Psalms* and the passages which I *have not* included. They are presented separately so that the difference in effect can be more clearly seen. First, the passages included earlier:

Psalm 90 (KJV)

1 Lord, thou hast been our dwelling place in all generations. 2 Before the mountains were brought forth, or even thou hadst formed the earth and the world, even from everlasting to everlasting, thou art God.

3 Thou sayest, "Return, ye children of men." 4 For a thousand years in thy sight are but as yesterday when it is past. 5 They are as a sleep. They are like grass which groweth up; in the morning it flourisheth, and groweth up; in the evening it withereth. 11 Who knoweth thy power? 12 So teach us to number our days that we may apply our hearts unto wisdom.

13 Return, O Lord. How long? 14 O satisfy us early with thy mercy that we may rejoice and be glad all our days. 16 Let thy work appear unto thy servants and thy glory unto their children; 17 and let the beauty of the Lord our God be upon us. Establish thou the work of our hands upon us; yea, the work of our hands establish it.

Now compare this selection with the verses or parts of verses which *have not* been included in *Silver in the Psalms*.

3 Thou turnest man to destruction. 5 Thou carriest them away as with a flood. 7 For we are consumed by thine anger, and by thy wrath are we troubled. 8 Thou hast set our iniquities before thee, our secret sins in the

light of thy countenance. 9 For all our days are passed away in thy wrath; we spend our years as a tale that is told. 10 The days of our years are threescore and ten, and if by reason of strength they be fourscore years, yet is their strength labor and sorrow, for it is soon cut off and we fly away. 11 Who knoweth the power of thine anger? Even according to thy fear, so is thy wrath. 13 Let it repent thee concerning thy servants. 15 Make us glad according to the days wherein thou hast afflicted us, and the years wherein we have seen evil.

As I have repeatedly said, the focus of my concern here is not with theology, but rather with the resulting feeling I am left with. In my version, I am left with the feeling of being taken care of by the eternal God of the universe who has all power. I am left with the awareness of the brevity of life and the importance of living life fully for God while I am here. In the passages which I did not include in my version, I am the object of God's wrath. Whether deservedly so or not is irrelevant; the feeling I experience is a hollow one which I do not like. Even with all the verses included there is yet a mixture of feeling. Both these latter results are contrary to the purpose I would have were I presenting this Scripture to bereaved persons suffering from the absence of a loved one.

So, I feel that another valuable use of the passages I have selected is their use on *special* occasions, for *special* purposes, particularly when positive feeling on the part of the hearers is the goal of the one reading the Scripture.

V. *Leaving Markers*

Another way to use *Silver in the Psalms* is to leave "markers." In this approach, one writes down in advance of his devotional reading what life problems he is experiencing at the present time. In doing this, perhaps you will be able to identify two or three, or even more. In the approach I am suggesting here, it is important not to begin reading until you have completed, as much as possible, your "problem survey."

After you have written down all the problems you are aware of in your life at the present time, number or code each of your problems in some easily recognizable way. For example, the symbol for problem number 1 could be a cross, and the symbol for problem number two could be a star. Other symbols you could use would be a circle, a triangle, a fish, any symbol of the Greek alphabet, etc. After you have devised your code system, begin to read in the Psalms, preferably beginning with Psalm 1.

As you read, look for passages which speak to you about your problems. When you find such a passage, place the number or code of your problem to which that particular psalm passage speaks and the date beside the psalm as a kind of "Ebenezer," your "Rock of Help," for you to remember through the years.

It is important that you not require that the passage *solve* your problem entirely before you place a mark there. Be content to mark the passage if, in some special way recognized by you, God has spoken to you in the passage. You'll know when this has happened by attending carefully to your feelings. When you feel comforted, encouraged, hopeful, more at ease and relaxed, this can be good evidence that God has indeed spoken to you.

I recognize, of course, that it is quite possible for you to read completely through the Psalms, never put down a mark indicating a recognized message to you, and yet feel quieted and peaceful. In such a case, one would *know* that God had spoken to him, even though he would find it very difficult to point exactly to the place where he had done so. But that is OK. Therapists know that nonspecific treatment is just as effective in many cases as specific treatment of a problem. Don't question—rejoice!

But most of the time you will be able to leave behind some "markers." When you've done this many times for many years, you will begin to see traces of blessings piling up all throughout the Psalms. Of course, what I have said here about the marking system can be applied to other parts of the Scripture, also. I feel, however, that perhaps the Psalms excel in their capacity to give such blessings, especially when arranged in the way I have done here.

VI. A Journal of Experiences

A spin-off benefit of the marking system I have just described is the system of keeping a personal journal. In the journal is compiled a list of the problems you have experienced through the years and a record of the specific passages which spoke to you when you had each of those particular problems. You have heard Christians tell how God used a particular passage to help them over a specific crisis in their lives. Such a testimony is beautiful. We would like to be able to share similar blessings if we could only remember them and be able to tell them.

I have a feeling that God's blessings are widely distributed among Christians, and that if a person would take the time to mark the passages that have helped him (and would correlate that help with a specific problem he had been experiencing), even the quietest and shyest of Christians would have much to give to everyone else at the personal level. They could tell other searchers at least what had been of help to them and the inquirer would then have at least something fairly concrete to go on as he searched for answers in his life.

One caution here: *Remember that what has helped you may not help someone else.* You should never expect some-

116

one else to be blessed by what blesses you. You can only *share* your blessing and see what happens. God has a whole world of media through which to bless. We need not pin him down to only a few—to ours.

VII. Relational Reading

I have mentioned several times the use the Psalms can be to help us focus in on our feeling life—a much neglected area for many of us. What this amounts to is what others have called "relational Bible study." Relational Bible study is a technique of studying the Scripture from the standpoint of where we are in our own daily lives. While it also seeks to identify spiritual truths or "the gospel" in the passages studied, there is an equal emphasis on examination of our feeling-response to the Scripture. We are asked to "get involved" in the biblical story or perhaps to *be* one of the characters for a while. That is, we are sometimes asked to identify so completely with the feelings and thoughts of one of the characters in the story we are studying that we could experience (to some degree) very much the same feelings that the person might have experienced. In this way we are able to achieve a much clearer understanding of the Bible character, and we are able to be more fully aware of the fact that some of the same things the Bible characters experienced, we too are experiencing right now. This makes the Bible real and as up-to-date as our present feelings.

Karl Olsson, a creative writer, has written perhaps the clearest statement of what relational Bible study is and how it can help us obtain even more from our Bible study. In his book, *Find Yourself in the Bible* (Minneapolis: Augsburg, 1974), subtitled "A Guide to Relational Bible Study for Small Groups," Dr. Olsson defined relational Bible studies as "studies designed to give the Bible a personal focus" (p. 11).

After recounting the experience he had which brought him

117

to the realization that the Bible is about relationships, he tells in more detail what that means to him for Bible study and for living:

"When accepted personally and relationally, the Bible through the work of the Spirit, continually creates new relationships. . . . It pushes me into an unending reassessment of my existence. . . . There are safer things than giving the Bible a personal, relational focus. Kierkegaard's story is not outdated. There is a room with two doors. Over one there is a sign, 'Heaven'; on the other a sign 'Lecture on Heaven.' And people flock through the door to the lecture. It is safer to keep the Bible an object. . . . If I let the Bible become God's voice speaking to me and working in me, there is no escape. . . . I am on my way into the risk and beauty of salvation" (pp. 30-31).

Dr Olsson identifies his indebtedness to his colleagues at Faith at Work as he sketches how relational Bible study speaks to four major kinds of relationships: to God; to self; to significant others; and to other people in the world. "To live relationally," he says, "is to risk meaningful interaction with all four" (p. 33).

Then, coming to his proposals for participating in meaningful relational Bible study, he suggests four principles which have proved helpful to him. (pp. 37-44). I have paraphrased them below and have discussed briefly what I understand Dr. Olsson to mean by each of them.

1. *Make the story your story.* This stresses that we must enter into the feeling lives of the characters and try our best to experience the incidents in their lives as if we were experiencing them ourselves.

2. *Identify with a character in the story.* This means the person in the story we *feel* closest to—whether or not that person is "noble."

3. *Find the gospel.* Dr. Olsson speaks of the gospel, viewed from the relational standpoint, as the "unbelievable truth that

118

God thinks each one of us important enough to come to us
. . . that he is willing to trust us even though we fail him
again and again" (p. 44).

4. *Give the story a name.* This means that one should
try to sum up the passage he has read by giving it a title or
some symbolic representation, such as a picture. He points
out that in so doing, we have a personal handle for the passage. This type of labeling or titling of a passage is very much
what I have suggested above as a way of making the Psalms
our own experience.

I think it is clear, from Dr. Olsson's concept of relational
Bible study, that many of the suggestions I have made about
how to use *Silver in the Psalms* are very much kin to the main
features of relational Bible study. I personally am indebted
to Karl Olsson and other Faith at Work staff members, such
as Ralph Osborne and Heidi Frost, for the awareness of the
method of relational Bible study as a special approach to the
study of the Scripture.

How then, more specifically, can we use relational Bible
study in our devotional use of *Silver in the Psalms*? Here
are some suggestions:

1. *Tune in to your feelings.* Get your mind set to respond
to what you read with your feelings. That means to set
aside the usual intellectual, categorical-type thinking. Try
not to: identify doctrine, look for a good outline for some
presentation, tie in the concept in the passage you are reading with a concept in some other part of the Scripture, or
count the number of times a word occurs. Instead, contin-
uously ask yourself what feeling you are experiencing.

2. *Tune in to your mental images.* Be fully aware of what
mental images come before your mind as you read a passage.
Is it an image of a place? Stop your reading, close your eyes,
and explore that place, asking God to show you what he
wants you to see. Is the image of another person? Notice in
your fantasy who that other person is, what he is doing, and

what he is saying. Ask God to tell you what it means. Is the image of yourself? Where are you in your fantasy? How old are you? Are you by yourself or with someone else? Who? Ask God to reveal to you what it all means.

3. *Let God speak to you.* Follow the suggestions made above on how to let God speak to you. Set your expectations so that you are confident that God will speak to you in this way if you will only get yourself ready to receive him.

There are few if any "stories" in *Silver in the Psalms.* Most of the historical and very personal elements have not been included in the selection. This increased ambiguity, as discussed in Part One, makes it easier for us to respond very personally with our feelings to the passages. It is easier to see ourselves.

I think it is now clear how reading the Psalms "relationally" through feeling can be yet another very fruitful way to use *Silver in the Psalms* in our devotional Bible reading. There is one additional way I have wanted to make a contribution to our appreciation of the Psalms through devotional Bible reading. This approach to blessing does not necessarily require the use of *Silver in the Psalms,* but it certainly does yield something beautiful, something good. This too I want to share.

VIII. Special Verses

The Psalms are precious to us, not only because they contain well-known psalms which have within them many beautiful verses gathered together in one place, but also because, scattered here and there throughout nearly all the psalms, there are pockets of silver for our souls. I have already set aside for special treatment sixteen psalms which are very rich in beauty. Many of them are stored in special memory tapes in our hearts. As we read them, they stir again our feelings and they become etched more deeply in our memory. The spiritual silver in the sixteen psalms is easy to mine—it lies at the surface.

I wanted, therefore, to try to collect many of the remaining pockets of silver, widely dispersed among the remaining psalms, so that they would be more available to us for our edification. Accordingly, I have collected several special verses from among the Psalms and grouped them together under a few broad headings. This will make them readily accessable to us.

It will be remembered that the psalms I had reserved for presentation in the King James Version included the following Psalms: 1, 8, 19, 23, 24, 27, 40, 46, 51, 90, 91, 100, 103, 118, 121, and 139. The verses which follow were selected from the remaining psalms. I have again chosen to present them in the King James Version because this is the version in which many of us have memorized them; it is the form in which we have them stored in our hearts. They are listed in numerical order by verse within each category.

The collection process was more important to me than the categories under which they are subsumed. I used pretty much the same process that I used in selecting passages for *Silver in the Psalms*. I listened carefully to my feeling, but I had a few other criteria for selection for use in this section. My purpose was not to collect all the verses I possibly could, but rather to include the best known, warmest verses which were positive in nature. While some verses which are included are not particularly well-known, they are included because they brought forth a special response in me. That is, I perceived something special and beautiful about these verses even though they may not be the most popular verses in the Psalms.

Since I had a smaller collection of verses than is contained in Part II, and since my criteria for selection were different than that used in Part II, I decided to keep the categories small in number. I arrived at five categories. Four of the categories were fairly easy to put together because they are rather homogenous, but one category is very broad. This is the first category which I am calling "Praise and Deliverance."

At first I attempted to divide this large category into two smaller ones. The separating principle was verses which dealt with praise as opposed to verses which dealt with feelings of protection and security. However, there were many marginal verses which would not fit appropriately into either category, but which would fit in well if they were combined. Thus, I decided to combine the two into one broad category. In order to have handled those marginal verses in some meaningful way, I would have had to create a great number of very small categories, or develop a miscellaneous category, which I did not want to do. Thus, since my purpose in this section was not so much categorizing as it was collecting verses, it was an easy choice for me to combine the two categories.

This category entitled "Praise and Deliverance" is made up of verses which reflect: praise to God, thanksgiving to God for many things—such as his readiness to forgive, his mercy, his compassion, his grace and patience; and verses which speak of the power of God, and the deliverance and protection he has provided through answered prayer. These verses reflect God's watchcare and guidance of us, and the consequent hope we posses as a result of his promises of protection and fulfillment in our lives. They contain verses which voice statement of self-encouragement. They reflect resolution of spirit to live the Christian life. In summary, they include a great number of the verses containing the theme we identify as being *the* major theme of the Psalms—praise and deliverance.

Psalm 4:8   I will both lay me down in peace, and sleep; for thou, Lord, only makest me dwell in safety.

Psalm 9:9	The Lord also will be a refuge for the oppressed, a refuge in times of trouble.
Psalm 17:8	Keep me as the apple of the eye, hide me under the shadow of thy wings.
Psalm 18:2	The Lord is my rock, and my fortress, and my deliverer; my God, my strength, in whom I will trust; my buckler, and the horn of my salvation, and my high tower.
Psalm 18:16	He sent from above, he took me, he drew me out of many waters.
Psalm 28:7	The Lord is my strength and my shield; my heart trusted in him, and I am helped: therefore, my heart greatly rejoiceth; and with my song will I praise him.
Psalm 31:20	Thou shalt hide them in the secret of thy presence from the pride of man; thou shalt keep them secretly in a pavilion from the strife of tongues.
Psalm 31:24	Be of good courage, and he shall strengthen your heart, all ye that hope in the Lord.
Psalm 32:7	Thou art my hiding place; thou shalt preserve me from trouble; thou shalt compass me about with songs of deliverance.
Psalm 32:8	I will instruct thee and teach thee in the way which thou shalt go: I will guide thee with mine eye.

Psalm 33:12	Blessed is the nation whose God is the Lord and the people he hath chosen for his own inheritance.
Psalm 33:18	Behold the eye of the Lord is upon them that fear him, upon them that hope in his mercy.
Psalm 34:7	The angel of the Lord encampeth round about them that fear him, and delivereth them.
Psalm 34:8	O taste and see that the Lord is good: blessed is the man who trusteth in him.
Psalm 34:15	The eyes of the Lord are upon the righteous, and his ears are open unto their cry.
Psalm 34:18	The Lord is nigh unto them that are of a broken heart; and saveth such as be of a contrite spirit.
Psalm 34:19	Many are the afflictions of the righteous: but the Lord delivereth him out of them all.
Psalm 36:7	How excellent is thy lovingkindness, O God! therefore the children of men put their trust under the shadow of thy wings.
Psalm 37:4	Delight thyself also in the Lord; and he shall give thee the desires of thine heart.
Psalm 37:5	Commit thy way unto the Lord; trust also in him; and he shall bring it to pass.
Psalm 37:7	Rest in the Lord, and wait patiently for

him; fret not thyself because of him who
prospereth in his way.

Psalm 37:25   I have been young, and now am old; yet
have I not seen the righteous forsaken, nor
his seed begging bread.

Psalm 42:2   My soul thirsteth for God, for the living
God: when shall I come and appear be-
fore God?

Psalm 42:5   Why art thou cast down, O my soul? Why
art thou disquieted in me? Hope thou in
God: for I shall yet praise him for the help
of his countenance.

Psalm 42:8   Yet the Lord will command his lovingkindness in the daytime, and in the night his
song shall be with me, and my prayer unto
the God of my life.

Psalm 50:10   For every beast of the forest is mine, and
the cattle upon a thousand hills.

Psalm 50:15   And call upon me in the day of trouble; I
will deliver thee, and thou shalt glorify me.

Psalm 55:22   Cast thy burden upon the Lord, and he
shall sustain thee; he shall never suffer
the righteous to be moved.

Psalm 56:3   What time I am afraid, I will trust in thee.

Psalm 57:7   My heart is fixed, my heart is fixed:
I will sing and give praise.

Psalm 56:11	In God have I put my trust; I will not be afraid of what man can do unto me.
Psalm 57:1	Be merciful unto me, O God, be merciful unto me: for my soul trusteth in thee: yea, in the shadow of thy wings will I make my refuge, until these calamities be over-past.
Psalm 61:2	From the end of the earth will I cry unto thee, when my heart is overwhelmed; lead me to the rock that is higher than I.
Psalm 62:5	My soul, wait thou only upon God; for my expectation is from him.
Psalm 63:7	Because thou hast been my help, therefore in the shadow of thy wings will I rejoice.
Psalm 63:8	My soul followeth hard after thee: thy right hand upholdeth me.
Psalm 66:1	Make a joyful noise unto God, all ye lands.
Psalm 66:8	O bless our God, ye people, and make the voice of his praise to be heard.
Psalm 66:19	But verily God hath heard me; he hath attended to the voice of my prayer.
Psalm 66:20	Blessed be God, who hath not turned away my prayer, nor his mercy from me.
Psalm 68:19	Blessed be the Lord, who daily loadeth us with benefit, even the God of our salvation.

Psalm 69:30	I will praise the name of God with a song, and will magnify him with thanksgiving.
Psalm 71:5	For thou art my hope, O Lord God: thou art my trust from my youth.
Psalm 72:19	And blessed be his glorious name for ever: and let the whole earth be filled with his glory. Amen, and Amen.
Psalm 73:25	Whom have I in heaven but thee? And there is none upon earth that I desire beside thee.
Psalm 75:1	Unto thee, O God, do we give thanks, unto thee do we give thanks: for that thy name is near thy wondrous works declare.
Psalm 84:11	For the Lord God is a sun and shield; the Lord will give grace and glory. No good thing will he withhold from them that walk uprightly.
Psalm 85:8	I will hear what God the Lord will speak, for he will speak peace unto his people, and to his saints.
Psalm 85:10	Mercy and truth are met together; righteousness and peace have kissed each other.
Psalm 85:11	Truth shall spring out of the earth; and righteousness shall look down from heaven.
Psalm 86:5	For thou, Lord, art good, and ready to forgive; and plenteous in mercy unto all them that call upon thee.

Psalm 86:7	In the day of my trouble I will call upon thee: for thou wilt answer me.
Psalm 86:10	For thou art great, and doest wondrous things: thou art God alone.
Psalm 86:12	I will praise thee, O Lord my God, with all my heart: and I will glorify thy name for evermore.
Psalm 86:15	But thou, O Lord, art a God full of compassion, and gracious, longsuffering, and plenteous in mercy and truth.
Psalm 89:1	I will sing of the mercies of the Lord for ever: with my mouth will I make known thy faithfulness to all generations.
Psalm 92:1-2	It is a good thing to give thanks unto the Lord, and to sing praises unto thy name, O most High, to shew forth thy lovingkindness in the morning, and thy faithfulness every night.
Psalm 95:1	O come, let us sing unto the Lord; let us make a joyful noise to the rock of our salvation.
Psalm 95:2	Let us come before his presence with thanksgiving, and make a joyful noise unto him with psalms.
Psalm 95:6	O come, let us worship and bow down: let us kneel before the Lord our maker.

Psalm 95:7	For he is our God; and we are the people of his pasture, and the sheep of his hand.
Psalm 96:1	O sing unto the Lord a new song; sing unto the Lord, all the earth.
Psalm 96:2	Sing unto the Lord, bless his name; shew forth his salvation from day to day.
Psalm 96:3	Declare his glory . . . his wonders among all people.
Psalm 96:4	For the Lord is great, and greatly to be praised.
Psalm 96:9	O worship the Lord in the beauty of holiness.
Psalm 97:6	The heavens declare his righteousness, and all the people see his glory.
Psalm 98:4	Make a joyful noise unto the Lord, all the earth: make a loud noise, and rejoice, and sing praise.
Psalm 104:33	I will sing unto the Lord as long as I live: I will sing praise to my God while I have my being.
Psalm 104:34	My meditation of him shall be sweet: I will be glad in the Lord.
Psalm 106:1	Praise ye the Lord. O give thanks unto the Lord; for he is good: for his mercy endureth for ever.

Psalm 107:8	Oh that men would praise the Lord for his goodness, and for his wonderful works to the children of men!
Psalm 107:9	He satisfieth the longing soul, and filleth the hungry soul with goodness.
Psalm 108:1	O God, my heart is fixed; I will sing and give praise, even with my glory.
Psalm 111:4	He hath made his wonderful works to be remembered; the Lord is gracious and full of compassion.
Psalm 111:10	The fear of the Lord is the beginning of wisdom: a good understanding have all they that do his commandments: his praise endureth.
Psalm 113:2	Blessed be the name of the Lord from this time forth and for evermore.
Psalm 113:3	From the rising of the sun unto the going down of the same, the Lord's name is to be praised.
Psalm 116:9	I will walk before the Lord in the land of the living.
Psalm 116:15	Precious in the sight of the Lord is the death of his saints.
Psalm 119:89	For ever, O Lord, thy word is settled in heaven.

Psalm 119:90	Thy faithfulness is unto all generations; thou hast established the earth, and it abideth.
Psalm 126:3	The Lord hath done great things for us; whereof we are glad.
Psalm 126:5	They that sow in tears shall reap in joy.
Psalm 126:6	He that goeth forth and weepeth, bearing precious seed, shall doubtless come again with rejoicing, bringing his sheaves with him.
Psalm 127:1	Except the Lord build the house, they labour in vain that build it: except the Lord keep the city, the watchman waketh but in vain.
Psalm 143:10	Teach me to do thy will, for thou art my God; thy spirit is good. Lead me into the land of uprightness.
Psalm 145:18	The Lord is nigh unto all them that call upon him, to all that call upon him in truth.
Psalm 146:2	While I live will I praise the Lord: I will sing praises unto my God while I have any being.
Psalm 147:3	He healeth the broken in heart, and bindeth up their wounds.
Psalm 150:6	Let every thing that hath breath praise the Lord. Praise ye the Lord.

The next set of verses centers around the theme of what the Christian would perceive as references to heaven or to the promised bliss for believers to be found in these verses. This set contains verses which allude to eternity and rescue from the grave. While heaven is not necessarily referred to directly, coming from the perceptual orientation of the Christian, heaven is clearly visible in these verses.

Psalm 4:3   But know that the Lord hath set apart him that is godly for himself.

Psalm 16:10   For thou wilt not leave my soul in hell; neither wilt thou suffer thine Holy One to see corruption.

Psalm 16:11   Thou wilt show me the path of life; in thy presence is fulness of joy; at thy right hand there are pleasures for evermore.

Psalm 17:15   As for me, I will behold thy face in righteousness; I shall be satisfied, when I awake, with thy likeness.

Psalm 25:14   The secret of the Lord is with them that fear him; and he will shew them his covenant.

Psalm 30:3   O Lord, thou hast brought up my soul from the grave: thou hast kept me alive, that I should not go down to the pit.

Psalm 30:5   Weeping may endure for a night, but joy cometh in the morning.

Psalm 31:5   Into thine hand I commit my spirit: thou

132

hast redeemed me, O Lord God of truth.

Psalm 31:19   Oh how great is thy goodness, which thou
hast laid up for them that fear thee; which
thou hast wrought for them that trust in thee
before the sons of men!

Psalm 37:11   But the meek shall inherit the earth, and
shall delight themselves in the abundance
of peace.

Psalm 37:18   The Lord knoweth the days of the upright,
and their inheritance shall be for ever.

Psalm 48:14   For this God is our God for ever and ever:
he will be our guide even unto death.

Psalm 49:15   But God will redeem my soul from the
power of the grave: for he shall receive me.

Psalm 50:5   Gather my saints together unto me; those
that have made a covenant with me.

Psalm 61:4   I will abide in thy tabernacle for ever:
I will trust in the covert of thy wings.

Psalm 72:17   His name shall endure for ever: his name
shall be continued as long as the sun: and
men shall be blessed in him: all nations
shall call him blessed.

Psalm 73:24   Thou shalt guide me with thy counsel, and
afterward receive me to glory.

Psalm 89:15   Blessed is the people that know the joyful

sound: they shall walk, O Lord, in the
light of thy countenance.

Psalm 92:13   Those that be planted in the house of the
Lord shall flourish in the courts of our God

Psalm 102:12   But thou, O Lord, shalt endure for ever;
and thy remembrance unto all generations.

Psalm 116:7   Return unto thy rest, O my soul; for the
Lord hath dealt bountifully with thee.

There are a great number of verses which deal with God's
word, his thoughts, his statutes, his law, his testimonies, and
other such references which trigger feelings about the Scriptures in the Christian. A great number of the verses are lo-
cated in Psalm 119, but there are other beautiful references
scatter throughout the Psalms. These are now collected
below.

Psalm 12:6   The words of the Lord are pure words: as
silver tried in a furnace of earth, purified
seven times.

Psalm 25:10   All the paths of the Lord are mercy and
truth unto such as keep his covenant and
his testimonies.

Psalm 33:4   The word of the Lord is right; and all his
works are done in truth.

Psalm 33:11   The counsel of the Lord standeth for ever,
the thoughts of his heart to all generations.

Psalm 105:8   He hath remembered his covenant for ever,

the word which he commanded to a
thousand generations.

Psalm 119:9   Wherewithal shall a young man cleanse his
way? by taking heed hereto according to
thy word.

Psalm 119:11   Thy Word have I hid in mine heart, that I
might not sin against thee.

Psalm 119:15   I will meditate in thy precepts and have
respect unto thy ways.

Psalm 119:16   I will delight myself in thy statutes: I
will not forget thy word.

Psalm 119:18   Open thou mine eyes, that I may behold
wondrous things out of thy law.

Psalm 119:27   Make me to understand the way of thy precepts: so shall I talk of thy wondrous works.

Psalm 119:97   O how love I thy law! it is my meditation
all the day.

Psalm 119:103 How sweet are thy words unto my taste!
yea, sweeter than honey to my mouth!

Psalm 119:105 Thy word is a lamp unto my feet, and a
light to my path.

Psalm 119:129 Thy testimonies are wonderful: therefore
doth my soul keep them.

Psalm 119:130 The entrance of thy words giveth light;

it giveth understanding to the simple.

Psalm 119:160   Thy word is true from the beginning and
                 every one of thy righteous judgments
                 endureth forever.

Psalm 119:165   Great peace have they who love thy law;
                 nothing shall offend them.

Several verses in the Psalms make reference to group worship and are reflected in such terms as congreagation, courts, sanctuary, tabernacle, palace, and assembly. They speak of worship and praise of God while together. The Christian, of course, would feel, while reading these verses, the fellowship of the church. Since *Silver in the Psalms* is based upon feeling, the categories are those of feeling. This feeling refers to the church. The verses which follow reflect such feelings, at least in me.

Psalm 34:3   O magnify the Lord with me, and let us
               exalt his name together.

Psalm 35:18   I will give thanks in the great congrega-
               tion: I will praise thee among much
               people.

Psalm 77:13   Thy way, O God, is in the sanctuary;
               who is so great a God as our God?

Psalm 84:1   How amiable are thy tabernalces, O Lord
               of hosts!

Psalm 84:2   My soul longeth, yea, even fainteth for
               the courts of the Lord: my heart and
               my flesh crieth out for the living God.

Psalm 84:10	For a day in thy courts is better than a thousand. I had rather be a doorkeeper in the house of my God, than to dwell in the tents of wickedness.
Psalm 89:7	God is greatly to be feared in the assembly of the saints, and to be had in reverence all them that are about him.
Psalm 96:8	Give unto the Lord the glory due unto his name: bring an offering, and come into his courts.
Psalm 111:1	Praise ye the Lord. I will praise the Lord with my whole heart, in the assembly of the upright, and in the congregation.
Psalm 116:14	I will pay my vows unto the Lord now in the presence of all his people.
Psalm 122:1	I was glad when they said unto me, Let us go into the house of the Lord.
Psalm 133:1	Behold, how good and how pleasant it is for brethren to dwell together in unity!
Psalm 134:2	Lift up your hands in the sanctuary, and bless the Lord.
Psalm 149:1	Praise ye the Lord. Sing unto the Lord a new song, and his praise in the congregation of saints.

Finally, there are six verses which make special reference to a very depleted human condition. They stir deep feelings within us and make our hearts go out to meet those needs. The verses speak of God's love and concern for the poor and the needy. Since verses like these evoke strong feelings of Christian charity and a responsibility to be our brother's keeper, at least at the level of needs, they are included in this last separate category.

Psalm 9:18	The needy shall not always be forgotten: the expectations of the poor shall not perish forever.
Psalm 10:17-18	Lord, thou hast heard the desire of the humble: thou wilt prepare their heart, thou wilt cause thine ear to hear: To judge the fatherless and the oppressed.
Palsm 41:1	Blessed is he that considereth the poor: the Lord will deliver him in time of trouble.
Psalm 72:12	For he shall deliver the needy when he crieth; the poor also, and him that hath no helper.
Psalm 72:13	He shall spare the poor and needy, and shall save the souls of the needy.

There is much more silver in the Psalms—if all were mined, I suppose that even the world could not contain the books that should be written!

APPENDIX
Subject Index